Nursing Leadership

Preparing for the 21st Century

American Organization of Nurse Executives

AHA

AHA books are published by American Hospital Publishing, Inc.,
an American Hospital Association company

Library of Congress Cataloging-in-Publication Data

Nursing leadership : preparing for the 21st century / American
    Organization of Nurse Executives : [Elizabeth Burkhart and Laura Skeggs,
    content editors].
        p.   cm.
    Includes bibliographical references.
    ISBN 1-55648-098-9 (pbk.)
    1. Nursing services—United States—Administration.
    2. Leadership. I. Burkhart, Elizabeth. II. Skeggs, Laura.
    III. American Organization of Nurse Executives.
        [DNLM: 1. Leadership—nurses' instruction. 2. Nursing—
        organization & administration—United States. WY 105 N97475]
    RT89.N795 1993
    362. 1'73'068—dc20
    DNLM/DLC
    for Library of Congress   92-49087
                                                 CIP

Catalog no. 154152

Printed in the USA

Text set in Palatino
4M—02/93—0338

Elizabeth Burkhart and Laura Skeggs, Content Editors
Audrey Kaufman, Acquisitions and Development Editor
Anne Hermann, Production Editor
Marcia Bottoms, Assistant Director
Peggy DuMais, Production Coordinator
Luke Smith, Cover Designer
Brian Schenk, Books Division Director

Contents

List of Figures and Tables

About the Authors

Martha Bermingham, R.N., M.M., is director of surgical nursing at Lutheran General Hospital in Park Ridge, Illinois. She has worked in different capacities in nursing for over 20 years, including staff, management, and consulting. Ms. Bermingham received her master's degree in management from the Kellogg Graduate School of Management, Northwestern University.

Susan Cummings, R.N., M.N., is president of Cummings Associates in San Diego, a group that provides health care and nursing consultation. In her former role as director of quality, education, and research at Sharp Memorial Hospital in San Diego, Ms. Cummings was actively involved in workplace redesign. A frequent speaker at national professional meetings, she has also coauthored numerous manuscripts about case management, staff empowerment, and workplace redesigns. Ms. Cummings received her bachelor of science degree in nursing from the University of Connecticut and her master's degree from the University of Washington.

Susanne DeFabiis, M.S., R.N., is a consultation/liaison clinical nurse at Christ Hospital in Oak Lawn, Illinois. She has been working in the field of consultation/liaison nursing for the past 15 years. Ms. DeFabiis also has experience as a nurse psychotherapist and as an instructor in nursing education. She received her master's degree from St. Xavier University in Chicago.

Vicki D. Lachman, R.N., Ph.D., is president of V. L. Associates, a health care consulting and training company in Philadelphia. She has given over 700 presentations and has done organizational analysis, team building, and leadership development consulting for more than 50 health care institutions. Dr. Lachman has written approximately 20 articles and several book chapters and is the author of *Stress Management: A Manual for Nurses,* published by W. B. Saunders in 1983. She was one of the presenters in the video, *AONE Nurse Management Survey Results.* Dr. Lachman received her Ph.D. from Temple University in Philadelphia.

Priscilla Lynch, M.S., R.N., is an assistant professor and unit leader at Rush-Presbyterian-St. Luke's Medical Center in Chicago, as well as a nurse psychotherapist at Oakside Clinic/Riverside Medical Center in Kankakee, Illinois. She has worked in the psychiatric nursing field for the past 15 years as a clinician, educator, and consultant. Ms. Lynch received her master's degree from St. Xavier University in Chicago.

Marie Manthey, R.N., M.N.A., is the president of Creative Nursing Management in Minneapolis, a full service consultation company specializing in professional practice, management training, staff empowerment, and work redesign. Her interest in the delivery of hospital services began in the sixties when she developed the concept of "Primary Nursing." Since then, Ms. Manthey has designed and implemented primary nursing programs for numerous hospitals. She has also conducted seminars on a variety of management and leadership topics for over 300,000 nurses. Prior to consulting, Ms. Manthey held positions in every level of nursing, from staff nurse to vice-president for patient services. Among her academic positions, she was associate professor at the University of Connecticut and associate clinical professor at Yale University School of Nursing. Ms. Manthey has written dozens of articles on nursing topics and is the author of *The Practice of Primary Nursing* (Cambridge, MA: Blackwell Scientific Publications Inc., 1980). She received her master's degree in Nursing Administration from the University of Minnesota.

James O'Malley, R.N., M.S., is a health care executive with a national reputation as a transformational leader. He is currently vice-president of patient care services at Sharp Healthcare in San Diego. In this position, he has redefined the role of the manager, implemented new care delivery and employee participation systems, and integrated diverse disciplines to best utilize employee skills and facilitate attainment of organizational outcomes for quality cost-effective care. Mr. O'Malley is a prolific writer, consultant, and lecturer. He is a frequent contributor to the nursing and health care literature and his award-winning video, *Nursing the Dance of Discipline,* has been shown on public television. Mr. O'Malley received his undergraduate degree from San Francisco State University and his graduate degree from Yale University.

Julie W. Schaffner, R.N., M.S.N., is vice-president of patient care services at Lutheran General Hospital in Park Ridge, Illinois. In this capacity, she is the designated chief nursing officer and is responsible for nursing and a number of professional and ancillary services. Ms. Schaffner serves on the editorial advisory board for the *Journal of Nursing Administration,* and has authored several articles. Ms. Schaffner is on the Rainbow Hospice and Neomedica/LGH Dialysis Center boards. She was previously with a "Big 8" accounting firm and labor relations firm. Ms. Schaffner received her master's degree in nursing from the University of Virginia.

Preface

Nursing operates at the center of today's fast-paced and constantly changing health care delivery system. To meet the seemingly inconsistent demands for quality, cost reduction, and reform, health care institutions are being restructured and patient care delivery systems redesigned. The patient population continues to age, and medical technology continues to expand. Overall, the health care needs of patients are increasingly greater.

Nursing roles also are shifting as different numbers and types of caregivers emerge. In the midst of all this change nursing management remains the linchpin in the health care organization, serving as the conduit between executive management and the bedside caregiver. Furthermore, nursing management ensures that patient needs are addressed in a way that is consistent with the organization's overall mission and operating philosophy.

To thrive and succeed today, nurse managers need enhanced understanding of key management skills and issues. The American Organization of Nurse Executives (AONE), as the nation's leadership organization for nurse executives and nurse managers, provides leadership, professional development, and advocacy in order to advance nursing practice and patient care and to promote nursing leadership excellence in its members. This book was derived from an educational program presented by AONE. It describes the key trends, issues, and skills needed by nursing management to promote organizational and personal excellence, inspire creativity, and achieve success in today's critical climate.

Chapter 1 discusses the need to empower nursing staff in order to create a professional practice environment and describes key leadership skills and strategies to accomplish that goal. Chapter 2 reviews the essential skills needed to manage change—delegation, conflict resolution, assertiveness, and negotiation. Chapter 3 examines how to create and maintain a high-performance team. The authors provide strategies for creating the right environment, employing and retaining the right people, and implementing the right processes to maximize performance while minimizing cost. Chapter 4 examines the issue of stress, a common component of change. Through various strategies and coping mechanisms, managers will learn how to help their staff (and themselves) manage stress in a positive manner. Finally, chapter 5 summarizes many of the current trends in, and implications of, redesigning care delivery. The discussion includes an overview of current popular models and describes a generic restructuring process.

The world of health care and health care management is changing rapidly. For nursing leaders with expanded insight and well-developed skills, these changes offer tremendous opportunities for growth, creativity, and innovation. It is AONE's hope that this book will inspire nursing management to foster the skills and mind-set to meet the challenges of nursing in the 21st century.

Carol M. Boston, J.D., M.S., R.N.
Executive Director
American Organization of Nurse Executives

Chapter 1

Empowering Staff to Create a Professional Practice Environment

Marie Manthey, R.N., M.N.A.

A professional practice environment empowers staff members to make decisions and take responsibility for them. Not only must management encourage and facilitate this kind of behavior from staff, but the organizational structure must support it. This chapter is divided into three sections. The first section focuses on leadership and identifies formal and informal nursing leaders. The second section describes professional practice and the organizational structure and culture that foster it. The third section provides strategies for empowering staff to create a professional practice.

□ Leadership

Leaders are people who influence others by what they say and how they say it. Leadership skills include creativity, influence, and the ability to apply vision to practice.

Leadership and management differ in the following ways—leaders lead people; managers manage organizations. Leaders influence, develop, and inspire; managers plan, control, direct, and evaluate. Although it is possible to be a leader and not a manager, it may not be possible to be an effective manager and not a leader. The manager's only choice is whether to be an effective leader or an ineffective leader.

Both leadership and management roles require learnable skills. Unfortunately, most nurse managers are promoted into their positions without adequate preparation in either area. A nurse manager is often selected because he or she has manifested some degree of organizational ability in handling staff responsibilities. It is seldom that anyone considers whether the candidate has leadership skills. Although leadership is neither evaluated nor required, it may be the most important qualification for managerial success. To ensure success, hospitals should provide both leadership and management training for nurse managers.

Formal Leaders

Nurse managers influence others as a result of their position of authority in the organization. The organizational structure gives managers the authority to exercise certain powers, including hiring, firing, evaluating, controlling, and rewarding staff. This is called "formal power." Managers who combine leadership skills with their managerial power and authority are "formal leaders."

Informal Leaders

Other staff members who influence people and have power are "informal leaders." Sometimes an informal leader is someone who expresses an opinion on everything, or he or she may be someone who changes other people's opinions by simply raising an eyebrow. How a nurse manager interacts with informal leaders will have an impact on his or her overall managerial effectiveness. Knowing who the informal leaders are and using their energy to enhance teamwork is a smart leadership technique. A method for identifying these people is discussed at the end of this chapter in the section on change through empowerment.

□ Professional Practice

Sociologists use certain characteristics of work activities to describe a professional. One of the most important of these characteristics is that the professional has an identifiable body of knowledge that forms the basis for making autonomous decisions in the particular field of endeavor. The quality of autonomous decision making is fundamental to any profession. The following section describes the key elements for a professional environment:

1. Decentralized authority
2. Empowered staff
3. Healthy interpersonal relations among staff
4. Unit culture that supports risk taking

Decentralized Authority

There are two styles of decision-making systems—centralized and decentralized. Knowledge is power, and, in centralized systems, only a few people know enough to make decisions. Routine matters are handled at the action level and the more difficult decisions at higher management levels. In decentralized systems, however, most decisions are made at the level of action.

Professional practice can exist only in decentralized systems. If top administrators believe that staff nurses are not able to manage patient care, professional practice will be difficult, if not impossible, to implement. However, when courageous nurse administrators and managers are willing to take the risks of decentralizing authority, professional practice is possible.

Decentralization can be implemented at the unit level through self-management teams, staff action committees, and/or other mechanisms for involving staff in operational decision making. One effective way to get this process started is to brainstorm to identify issues on which the staff would like to work, practices they would like to improve, or problems they would like to solve. Once issues, goals, or problems have been identified and prioritized, task forces can be appointed to address each topic. For example, committees can be appointed to develop staffing schedules, patient care delivery models, or unit-based quality assurance mechanisms. For maximum effectiveness, the nurse manager must be sure that each group has the ability *and* the authority to effectively deal with the issues.

Empowered Staff

Professional practice requires individuals to accept responsibility for their actions and to act with personal authority. Managers who are effective leaders can create an environment for professional practice by guiding staff empowerment.

Empowerment means taking the responsibility to change one's environment. An empowered person must be able to function as a "responsible adult," that is, be able to accept responsibility for his or her actions. Personal power is only accessed as a by-product of accepting responsibility. Many people experience a deep-seated reluctance to accept responsibility for their own life experiences, resulting in feelings of victimization. People who feel victimized are often unable to see that by accepting responsibility for their own experiences, they will have access to choices and open the door to empowerment.

As mentioned previously, empowerment depends on the individual's ability to make decisions at the action level. For this to happen, staff functions must be organized around a process consisting of three sequential elements—responsibility, authority, and accountability. First, professional nurses establish responsible relationships with their patients. Second, professional nurses exercise authority for managing their patients' nursing care. Third, by exercising authority, nurses can be held accountable for the quality of their decisions regarding patient care.

Responsibility

The derivation of the word *responsibility* deals with the ability to respond, hence "response ability." In an organizational structure, there are two components to consider—responsibility allocation and responsibility acceptance. For these components to be functional, they must be clear and visible within the system. Everybody must know who is responsible for what and when.

In a hierarchical system, individuals higher in the organizational structure can legitimately assign responsibility to their staff. This is called the legitimate chain of command. For example, the board of trustees assigns responsibility to the chief executive officer (CEO) of the hospital, and, in turn, the CEO allocates responsibility to the vice-president of nursing. For the system to work effectively, the allocatee must accept responsibility from the allocator. However, just because a manager assigns responsibility does not mean that a staff member accepts that responsibility. Many nurses are reluctant to accept responsibility for managing patient care because they fear being blamed if something goes wrong. One of the greatest challenges facing nursing today is developing staff nurses who are willing and able to accept responsibility for managing patients' care. "He's not my patient!" is still one of the most common responses heard to queries about a problem in patient care.

In order to practice professionally, a nurse needs to establish responsible relationships with his or her patient. The patient must know the name of the nurse and the level of his or her responsibility related to the patient's care. Visible acceptance of responsibility is an essential prerequisite to acquiring the necessary authority to manage care. When patients, their families, and others in the system, including physicians and other nurses, know the name of the responsible nurse, conditions for professional autonomy are in place.

Authority

Authority is the right to act in an area in which one has been delegated and has accepted responsibility. Along with delegating responsibility, managers must allocate the legitimate authority to take action, and staff must accept responsibility for this power. Authority also can be viewed as a by-product of accepting responsibility. Nurses must accept responsibility before they can experience legitimate authority to practice professionally.

Accountability

Accountability is the retrospective review of work to determine whether it met prescribed standards of care. Again, the process is sequential. Professional accountability follows the acceptance of responsibility and the exercising of legitimate authority. Accountability mechanisms usually involve a structured evaluation procedure that compares performance with practice or care standards. If nursing care does not meet the standards, corrective action should be taken.

Accountability is a professional obligation. There are two common mechanisms to measure accountability—institution-based employee evaluation tools and standard-based clinical monitors. There is a wide range of choices for both types of measurement. Employee evaluation systems range from detailed pay-for-performance systems, to loosely designed, open-ended progress reports. Self-evaluation, peer evaluation, and supervisor evaluations are also options. Quality assurance systems are also plentiful. Standard-based evaluation systems are derived from the minimum quality assurance requirements of the Joint Commission on Accreditation of Healthcare Organizations (JCAHO). In response to JCAHO requirements, many hospitals have developed outcome criteria–based care standards. When quality becomes an organizational mission, professional accountability is greatly enhanced.

As discussed, responsibility, authority, and accountability are the steps to empowerment. From an organizational perspective, these three elements shape the basis of functional job descriptions from staff nurses to executive management and provide the structure for a professional practice. From a personal perspective, they assist individuals in achieving the empowerment necessary for professional practice.

Healthy Interpersonal Relations

In most cases, nurses working at the unit level do not, of their own volition, set up effective harmonious teams. The nurse manager should help the staff develop confidence and provide guidance in building healthy interpersonal relationships. Two specific strategies for creating and managing healthy working relationships are discussed later in this chapter.

Unit Culture That Supports Risk Taking

In order to create a professional practice environment, the basic culture of a nursing unit should support healthy interpersonal relationships, facilitate problem solving, and encourage appropriate risk taking. However, the present way the staff interacts, their feelings about the unit and each other, and the language used by both nursing and other team members may reinforce dependent or unempowered behaviors. There-fore, it may be necessary for the unit culture change in order to pro-mote a professional practice environment in which risk taking is not feared. A strategy for changing the unit culture is described in the next section.

☐ Strategies for Empowering Staff to Create a Professional Practice

Creating a professional practice environment requires work, persever-ance, and faith. This section describes three strategies for empowering staff to create a professional practice. Depending on the organization and its particular environment, managers may choose to implement one, two, or all three of the following strategies:

- A framework for empowerment shows managers how applying partic-ular leadership skills will enhance a professional practice environment.
- The 10 practical steps in developing a professional staff supports the framework for empowerment.
- Change through empowerment facilitates a culturewide transformation.

Framework for Empowerment

The framework for empowerment, illustrated in figure 1-1, articulates the major issues universal to professional nursing. The overall components of this model include articulating expectations, enhancing staff skills needed for successful empowerment, and developing management skills necessary for facilitating staff empowerment. The major areas in which staff are generally deficient include solving problems, managing rela-tionships, and taking risks. In order to promote the staff's learning and growth, managers must develop skills such as consensus building, con-flict resolution, and discipline without punishment.

Articulate Expectations

Traditional management control techniques are inappropriate when managing a professional staff. Many people can remember traditional head nurses who made rounds with the physician and seemed to be an expert on all patient care issues. They were traffic directors and clini-cal decision makers, the ones everyone sought for answers to their ques-tions. Because this type of control stifles growth, nurse managers must learn to allow their staff to grow. The absence of traditional controls, however, can create a vacuum unless replaced with strong leadership

Figure 1-1.   Framework for Empowerment

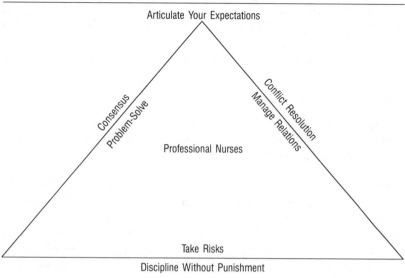

Articulate Your Expectations

Consensus
Problem-Solve

Conflict Resolution
Manage Relations

Professional Nurses

Take Risks
Discipline Without Punishment

techniques. Articulating expectations is such a technique. By the nurse manager's articulating his or her expectations, everyone knows what they are expected to accomplish. As a result, the nurse manager has embodied, or role modeled, the kind of clear communication expected among the staff. There is no more "mind reading what the boss wants."

This step is most effective when implemented in a one-on-group communication—in monthly staff meetings, for example. The format of these meetings should support the unit's positive accomplishments. Expectations usually cover clinical, as well as work group, issues. To be successful, expectations need to be relevant, realistic, achievable, and acceptable. If the nurse manager's expectations are irrelevant, such as expecting a 45-minute assessment on each patient during each shift, he or she will lose credibility as a leader. If the nurse manager's expectations are unrealistic (expecting every physician to say "our unit is the best"), or unachievable (expecting every registered nurse to enroll in a baccalaureate program), or unacceptable (expecting all nurses to assist with abortions), his or her leadership role will be weakened. As a first step, and as a continual process, communicating expectations must be carefully planned and thoughtfully executed. Realistic expectations may include the following:

- Patients know the name of the nurse who has overall (24-hour-per-day) responsibility for managing their care.

- Primary nurses communicate care decisions in writing for others to follow in their absence.
- Patients are prepared for discharge, with planning starting as soon after admission as is practical.
- Staff members come to work on time and are appropriately dressed.

Provide Staff with Skills Enhancement

The essential skills that lead to empowerment are relationship management, problem solving, and appropriate risk taking. Nurse managers should encourage and facilitate the acquisition of these skills.

Problem Solving

The process of solving problems is similar to that of decision making. A series of steps must be taken to identify alternatives for selecting an action and solving or modifying a problem area. Nurses deal with highly complex situations involving large quantities of scientific and technical data. In this arena the boundaries of authority are often ambiguous. The transition from the protected environment of the student nurse to the real world of nursing with all its complications is fraught with dangers. Not only may nurses not know everything they need to know in these situations, but often they are unclear as to their level of responsibility. For example, it will make a difference in terms of physician response whether the medical issues are strictly nursing. Policies, regulations, and laws add to the layers of complexity and danger. As a result, many nurses are not comfortable making decisions. Therefore, nurse managers must be prepared to teach staff nurses how to solve problems effectively.

An important aspect of problem solving is to define who owns a problem. The owner is the person who is affected by the problem, and her or she must deal with it. Asking someone else (such as the nurse manager) to deal with an uncomfortable situation is shirking one's responsibility. Nurse managers who allow staff to pass problems along to them for solution end up infantalizing, rather than empowering, that staff.

Another part of problem solving is to define the problem itself. Once defined, most problems are easily solved using available resources, such as reading reference books, consulting clinical department staff, or seeking professional assistance. Educational programs, multidisciplinary conferences, and staff meetings can also be helpful in problem solving.

Relationship Management

Healthy interpersonal relationships, characterized by open communication, trust, and mutual respect, are essential for a professional practice unit. A unit's goal should be that 100 percent of the staff have healthy relationships with each other. It is unacceptable for there to be shift-to-shift tensions, old timer against newcomer friction, cliques, anger, ridicule, and/or other dysfunctional communication. By establishing the following principle, nurse managers will teach staff how to manage their interpersonal relationships: If anyone on this unit is having a problem with anyone else, he or she is responsible for solving it with that person. Third parties may be used for advice or counsel only.

Ideally, nurses should be able to manage their relationships without help from the nurse manager. Communication skills training is one of the most important obligations of a leader in modern nursing. Therefore, the nurse manager must provide opportunities for staff to practice effective learning techniques with each other. Inservice classes with role playing, assertiveness books, one-on-one coaching sessions, and communication videos are all helpful teaching tools.

Risk Taking
In nursing the universal fear of making a mistake is closely related to nurses' lack of effective problem-solving skills. Because nurses were taught to maintain a zero-tolerance for error, most do not acknowledge the reality of human imperfection. Because a nurse error may harm a patient, nurses strongly dread making a mistake. This situation is compounded by a history in health care of using punishment to cause emotional pain in order to prevent mistakes from recurring. The outcome of this policy results in nurses' deep-seated reluctance to engage in decision making regarding patient care. To change this pattern, managers should create an environment for risk taking – rewarding risk takers and not punishing those who make mistakes. Methods to assist safe risk taking will be further explored later in this chapter.

Acquire the Appropriate Management Skills

Along with providing staff with problem-solving, relationship-managing, and risk-taking skills, nurse managers need to focus on their own skills in the following areas:

- Consensus building
- Conflict resolution
- Discipline without punishment

Consensus Building
When decisions need to be made that will affect the unit's practice of nursing, a consultative process is better than an autocratic one. Decisions made by consensus are the best way to safeguard autonomy within a unit.

However, formal voting on issues is best avoided. It is counterproductive to teamwork and tends to polarize staff.

A consensus-based decision, on the other hand, is a negotiated agreement. A negotiated agreement can be achieved by polling members of a group informally, if the issue is not controversial, or by facilitating discussion and allowing the group to come to a consensus. In this manner of consensus building, there are no winners or losers. Everyone compromises and agrees to a mutual decision. At the conclusion of such a process, all those involved should be able to say:

- "I believe I understand each person's position."
- "I believe each of you understands my position."
- "Whether or not I agree with the decision, I will support it because I believe it was arrived at fairly and openly."

Conflict Resolution

As staff members become better able to manage their relationships with each other, nurse managers need to complement these growing skills with the art of conflict resolution. A skilled conflict manager, rather than intervening with a decision about who is right and who is wrong, can implement a process that enables both parties together to choose how to solve their problem. In this way, the conflicting staff members maintain responsibility for managing themselves. At the same time, the nurse manager is able to facilitate solutions to serious problems.

When emotions run high, communication can easily become warped. An effective manager might ask both parties to state their version of what happened and then to repeat what each believes the other has said. In this way, communication barriers are often removed and problems eliminated. Specific conflict resolution strategies, including the use of assertiveness and negotiation techniques to promote win–win situations, are discussed in chapter 2.

Discipline without Punishment

Historically, nurses have not tolerated mistakes—even mistakes that were not preventable or predictable. Management's response to problems is often based on the notion that if people feel badly enough this time, they will not make another mistake next time. Because they were afraid of punishment, few nurses were willing to take risks.

To support the level of risk taking inherent in judgment-based decision making, nurse managers must be skilled in the art of discipline without punishment. This approach focuses on correcting problems without intentionally causing pain whether in the form of shame or guilt.

In a professional practice environment, mistakes must be viewed as a normal component of human interactions. Many hospitals are reviewing and revising personnel policies to incorporate the concept of discipline without punishment. Every nurse manager needs to examine his or her own management style to determine whether he or she incorporates the use of punishment into disciplinary actions. Separating punishment (causing pain) and discipline (teaching, learning) is vital in reformulating the processes used to respond to mistakes.

Nurse managers should first identify the cause of an error and then take the appropriate corrective action. For example, if a medication error was caused by a nurse's lack of knowledge or skill, the nurse manager's appropriate response is to teach the individual what he or she needs to know to prevent such an error from recurring.

Teaching should not be done in a punitive, shame-based manner. (For example, the nurse manager should not say, "I don't know what they teach you any more. It seems as though I have to teach you everything.") Using discipline without punishment simply involves straightforward education without critical comments. If a nurse's attitudinal problem causes the mistake, the nurse manager should formally develop and communicate acceptable behavior expectations and discuss them with the nurse, using a timetable to ensure future patient safety. If the mistake is caused by a systems error, the nurse manager should work with upper management and middle managers to change the system to eliminate the errors. Mistakes that are not the result of a knowledge or skill deficiency, attitudinal difficulties, or system problems can be thought of as human error. They occur because we *are* human and, therefore, not perfect. The appropriate management technique for this type of error is forgiveness.

Discipline without punishment represents a paradigm shift for most nurses and for many parts of the health care system. Many policies and official responses to mistakes are still punitive. Nurse managers should work through the system to eliminate these archaic policies.

10 Practical Steps to Develop a Professional Staff

Nurse managers who start with step 1 and follow through to step 10 will be well on the way to developing a professional practice environment:

1. *Assess the strengths and weaknesses of each staff member,* evaluating clinical practice capabilities and ability to function independently. As a manager, it is imperative that you know the competency level of all the people who report to you. Write a few phrases by each staff member's name describing your assessment of his or her abilities and deficiencies.
2. *Establish your role as a clinical resource.* Encourage strong staff members to use their expertise instead of abdicating their clinical decision-

making power. Be available. Validate, support, and recognize exemplary practice while fostering independence and autonomy. To serve as a clinical resource, you need to know the patients. Make rounds regularly to establish and maintain your own relationship with patients. Be interested and helpful as your nurses try to solve problems.

3. *Maximize human resources.* Develop strategies to develop and enhance the strengths of individual nurses. If one nurse is strong in gerontology, ask him or her to teach a class. If another is good with colostomy care, see whether he or she is willing to be a consultant to other nurses. At the same time, develop strategies to overcome clinical and interpersonal relationship weaknesses. It is not enough to simply know your nurses' individual weaknesses. It is the nurse manager's job to develop experiential and educational growth opportunities for each individual.

4. *Encourage staff to develop decision-making and problem-solving skills.* Provide effective and accessible problem-solving techniques. Identifying and discussing problems with the individuals involved can be highly effective in solving problems. Use problem-solving techniques often in your discussions about patient care. If you want effective professionals, encourage them to be top-notch problem solvers.

5. *Encourage staff to develop communication skills in order to manage their own interpersonal relationships.* First-person communication is essential to good teamwork. Role modeling and coaching are two effective ways to improve communication skills among staff members. Nurse managers must learn to avoid "taking the monkey on their backs." When staff members cannot rely on the manager to fix their relationship issues, they learn how to do it themselves.

6. *Become skilled in conflict resolution techniques*—including assertiveness and negotiation to promote win–win situations—to assist staff members in solving their own interpersonal problems. The use of conflict resolution techniques enables staff members to solve their own problems and facilitates empowerment even when severe problems exist.

7. *Establish an atmosphere that is safe for risk taking.* Talk about potential pitfalls before they come up. This will help dissipate some of the fear of risk taking. As you encourage decision making, assure staff that you trust their judgment. (However, if you do not trust their judgment, create a plan to increase their skill level.) Tell them to do the best they can and assure them that you will support them and follow through.

8. *Determine the cause of the error.* Differentiate between human errors (those that are neither preventable nor predictable) and mistakes requiring corrective action (deficiencies in knowledge or skill, attitudinal problems, and systems or design deficiencies). Investigate the circumstances of each mistake carefully, without seeking to fix blame.

9. *Develop an understanding of the difference between discipline and punishment.* The root of the word *punish* is penalty. The root of the word *discipline* is learning. Historically, nurse managers have relied on pain (penalty) as a way to prevent the nurse from repeating a mistake. However, mistakes need correction, not punishment.
10. *Become skilled in using nonpunitive disciplinary measures.* Use the discipline-without-punishment strategies previously described in this chapter. Whatever the reason for the mistake, make sure there is no effort on anyone's part to cause the individual to feel shame or guilt. Such painful feelings are part of the punishment paradigm. If the mistake was not caused by a knowledge or skill deficiency, a behavioral problem, or a system failure, it may belong to the category of human error. The appropriate response in this case is forgiveness.

Change through Empowerment

The interrelated change and empowerment processes can create powerful synergy under certain circumstances. Empowering staff may require changes in the hospital's management structure and environment. Once staff members are empowered, they may wish to change hospital policies, procedures, and systems further. With these hospitalwide changes, more staff become empowered, and soon cyclically, continually, create a more empowered, professional practice environment. It is imperative that nurse leaders manage this change effectively in order to facilitate empowerment and growth among the whole staff.

The resistance of staff nurses to accepting responsibility for their clinical practice is one of the major impediments to professional practice. They are often uncomfortable making decisions and then being held accountable for those decisions. Until that hurdle is overcome, staff will not become empowered and autonomous patient care decisions will not be a regular feature of nursing practice. Personal empowerment is essential for professional practice.

The strategy described here facilitates the change in culture that fosters personal empowerment. This process is not for the fainthearted. It requires a leap of faith and the courage to keep moving forward throughout a complex, profound process of change.

The process for empowering the staff is as important as the outcome. The manager's role in this process is critical. It is analogous to the role of an attending physician when a new batch of interns and residents enters the medical center. The manager should be supportive but not controlling, distant enough to be unavailable to provide staff an easy way out and yet close enough to be an effective cheerleader.

Change through empowerment means using the need for change as an opportunity to reconfigure a unit's culture positively. Team building, where decisions affecting the unit's operations are made by consensus, is used to involve the informal leaders in healthy interactions. This process also requires the development of a communications network that allows for input from and feedback to the entire staff.

The four elements of a successful change-through-empowerment process are:

1. Identifying the core group of informal leaders and other members who will be involved in the project
2. Developing a group with healthy interpersonal relationships
3. Creating a tightly linked network between the core group and the rest of the staff
4. Making consensus-based decisions about aspects of unit operations that affect the entire staff

Identify the Core Group

In order for the nurse manager to successfully capitalize on the energies of informal leaders, the leaders must be members of the core group. Successful change through empowerment is only possible when the staff's "informal influencers" are on the core committee. The nurse manager may believe he or she knows who these people are, but experience has shown that the real informal leaders are not always visible. The only foolproof way to identify informal leaders is by asking the entire staff to submit the names of the people they would like to see on the core committee. The nurse manager should not limit the process in any way; that is, not asking them to submit names in various employment categories (registered nurse, licensed practical nurse, nurse assistant) or names according to shift, tenure, education, or any other defining characteristic. This group should consist of 8 to 12 members. If fewer individuals surface as leaders, other staff members should be added. However, the nurse manager must not eliminate any of the informal leaders. The core group should also represent those who support change and those who do not. Success depends on having all interests of the staff represented, not necessarily all job categories, shifts, or educational levels.

Organize the Group

The purpose of this step is to develop the "aggregate of people" into a decision-making group and to establish and maintain healthy interpersonal relationships among members. Although this group process revolves around problem solving, it is important for the nurse manager to remember that the purpose of the process is to create a cohesive group with healthy interpersonal relationships.

Group Formation
To facilitate group formation, it is appropriate for the nurse manager to be present at the first meeting. After that, the nurse manager's role should be that of coach, cheerleader, and advisor. It usually makes sense for the nurse manager to schedule the first meeting in which he or she sets forth the following tasks:

- Giving the explicit charge to the group, including what they can decide and what they can recommend. The tasks may vary from changing shift reports to changing the delivery system. Whatever the assignment, the nurse manager must be clear about the group's level of authority. The nurse manager must not renege on the commitment to change.
- Helping the group select a chairperson or cochairpeople.
- Setting the dates and times for the next eight meetings. That is usually enough to get the work done and gives staff a realistic expectation of the time involved. If more time is needed, additional meetings can be scheduled at the end of the planning period.
- Beginning some group formation activities, if there is time and it seems appropriate. One such activity is to have a group member start a discussion by answering the following four questions:
  - Why did I become a nurse in the first place?
  - What kind of patients do I most like to care for?
  - What frustrates me most around here?
  - In what way does my position meet my original objectives?

If the nurse manager is likely to become defensive, it is better to have the chairperson lead the group in discussing these questions.

There are two common outcomes to this organizing phase. One is that the group begins to identify their similarities and differences. People find out that while one nurse prefers caring for elderly women, another really likes people her own age. It will become apparent that nearly everyone particularly enjoys caring for one type of patient. It is also interesting to discover that often at least one staff person appears to care for every type of patient on a unit. Another outcome is that people begin to focus on the difference between their ideals about nursing and nursing in reality. Although this difference can be discouraging, it can also be the a primary motivator for change. This simple discussion process can often effectively "unfreeze" attitudes and reduce resistance to positive change.

Maintenance of Healthy Relationships
One of the biggest challenges for the nurse manager is maintaining healthy group relationships over time. Sometimes groups shut down

because of internal strife or conflict. It is vital that relationship problems be solved. Otherwise, the process will be ineffective and the staff will feel more defeated than before the process started.

Two common personalities that can create problems in a group are the intimidators and the perfectionists. The intimidator threatens and the perfectionist assigns guilt. People who feel threatened or guilty are not going to risk speaking up. The group needs to learn how to deal with these behavior problems. The controlled environment in a small group offers a perfect opportunity for staff to overcome such problems. The best way to deal with difficult behavior issues is to have an expert in group processes available to help the group learn to cope with these problems. A psychiatric nurse, social worker, chaplain, or staff development nurse can be used as a consultant to the committee.

As the informal leaders learn how to cope with these problems, they will begin to utilize their new skills outside of the group as well. Thus, as problem behaviors are handled, staff morale overall should begin to improve.

Develop a Tight Communication Network

Establishing a tight communication network between the planning group and the rest of the staff is the mechanism for leveraging the culture change. By maintaining a tight network, the informal leaders influence the entire group directly. Each member of the committee should have the names of three or four members of the staff whom they regularly inform of the group's progress. It is important that the group be seen as a planning committee and not as a secret society. The more the committee members inform and poll the staff, the more the staff will accept the core committee's decisions. Committee members should contact their staff links before a meeting to ask for recommendations on key issues. The committee members should also contact them after the meeting to report on the decisions made. The tighter the communication network is drawn, the more effective the process will be.

Make Consensus-Based Decisions

Consensus means collectively making a judgment or coming to a conclusion. Decisions made using a consensus-based process usually reflect a negotiated, if not a unanimous, agreement. When the core committee has studied an issue and is ready to decide on a solution, a consensus-based decision will facilitate true empowerment more effectively than any other problem-solving or decision-making approach.

When an empowered group reaches consensus, management and the rest of the staff must accept and implement the decision or else the process will have very negative results. Staff will lose both faith and hope—faith in the nurse manager as a leader and hope for their own professional growth in that environment. That is why the charge to the group must be carefully developed and the nurse manager must be clear about the group's decision-making authority.

This process works independently of individual issues. The group can use this process to redesign care delivery on the unit or to change the shift report; the group can decide how to schedule lunch breaks or to change how to schedule time. However, if the group's decisions become mere recommendations, the process may fall short of a true empowerment experience.

As discussed earlier, consensus decisions require negotiation and discussion, rather than voting. Although everyone may not agree with the final decision, all staff should be willing to comply with it. Consensus-based decisions are critically important for the overall success of the empowerment process.

☐ Conclusion

The process of empowering staff requires implementing new skills and strategies for staff and management, having faith in the abilities of individuals, maintaining healthy group dynamics, and having a willingness to take chances. Only through effective leadership can managers empower their staffs in order to create a professional environment.

Chapter 2

Acquiring Key Skills in Managing Change

Vicki D. Lachman, R.N., Ph.D.

Redesigning the health care system will continue to cause role changes at every level of the health care hierarchy. As organizations continue to decentralize and as staff members assume increased decision-making responsibility, it becomes crucial that nurse managers continually clarify their expectations of employees, coworkers, and upper-level managers.

Responsibility and accountability issues surface naturally as roles change. A lack of role clarity can create duplication of work and turf battles, often leaving staff members feeling frustrated, resentful, and unappreciated. Roles are one of the key ways individuals define their interpersonal relationships. Therefore, when roles change, the dynamics of interpersonal relationships also change. For example, many licensed practical nurses (LPNs) and nurse aides (NAs) who have had their own patient assignments for years may suddenly find themselves assigned only to specific tasks—such as taking vital signs, transporting patients, and doing bed baths. This role change affects not only their own responsibilities, but also their relationships with the registered nurses (RNs). Licensed practical nurses and nurse aides frequently feel demoted. Staff nurses in differentiated practice and case management models can also feel demoted. Therefore, it is important that nurse managers have the skills to help all staff feel that they are important members of the nursing unit team. The four basic skills needed to accomplish this objective are: delegation, conflict resolution, assertiveness, and negotiation.

A well-functioning nursing unit team can be compared with a winning sports team. On a unit staff team, nurse managers are coaches. They meet with their team during the change-of-shift report, in staff meetings, and at other times when members need guidance. Nurse managers spend most of their time with their "quarterbacks" (primary nurses,

case managers, council chairpersons, and other registered nurses held
accountable for patient care and other management functions on the unit)
who guide the other team members. Quarterbacks are responsible for
designing and communicating the plan of care to all members of their
teams. Team members are responsible for implementing the plan and
bringing care issues to the quarterbacks' attention. Registered nurse quarterbacks call the plays, but in order to develop the best plan, they also
need feedback from their team members and their nurse manager
coaches.

This analogy demonstrates the importance of using all members of
the team effectively to foster a collaborative climate. The nurse manager
coaches and guides the staff in utilizing appropriate team members for
tasks and projects on the unit. Through the process of delegation, the
team learns each member's strengths. When team members fail to delegate or to complete their delegated assignments, conflict may arise. Effective follow-up requires the nurse manager to promote conflict resolution,
assertiveness, and negotiating skills. The four skills discussed in this
chapter are crucial to maintaining a well-functioning team that provides
high-quality patient care.

☐ Delegation

The structure of any organization is determined by four management
decisions: division of labor, the way work is divided; departmentaliza-
tion, the way jobs are grouped (for example, by function, geography,
product/service, customer served, or mixture of these); span of control,
the amount of contact between manager and employees; and delegation, the method by which decision-making authority is distributed
among jobs.[1]

In the past, the organizational structure was determined at the executive level. In current practice, nurse executives often involve their nursing team in determining the structure of the nursing department. Nurse
managers can participate in any of the four management decisions.
However, they should always participate in decisions involving delegation, because delegation is the primary method linking the organization's
needs with the individuals who actually do the work.

Delegation is the assignment of responsibility to others, commensurate with their training and experience. Delegation ensures the effective functioning of the organization and enhances individual
development.[2] It is the process of assigning responsibility and cor-
responding authority to specific individuals and then holding them
accountable for their performance. Delegation is not a "one-way street";
it is a contract whereby two parties come to an agreement. The following

subsections describe the legal, regulatory, and policy issues surrounding delegation, as well as how to delegate effectively.

Legal, Regulatory, and Policy Issues

The state nurse practice act, the state board of nursing regulations, and the policies established by the individual institution define the degree and type of delegation allowed. Each state defines in its nurse practice act and board of nursing regulations what activities registered nurses can legally delegate. In addition, within the boundaries of state law, each hospital defines in its policies, procedures, job descriptions, and what specific activities registered nurses can legally delegate.

For example, in Pennsylvania licensed practical nurses can administer intravenous (IV) medications according to the Pennsylvania Board of Nursing's regulations. However, prior to being certified by the institution as competent in that skill, they must meet clinical and educational requirements in IV administration. The Pennsylvania Nurse Practice Act and the Board of Nursing regulations say that licensed practical nurses may administer IV medications as part of their jobs. However, some institutions do not adopt that as institutional policy. Therefore, when employed by these institutions, licensed practical nurses may not legally administer IV medications.

The steps in designing a job description that is within legal boundaries are as follows:

1. Request from the state board of nursing a copy of the nurse practice act and all regulation changes.
2. Request from the personnel department the most recent job descriptions, the union policy handbook (if applicable), and a job evaluation form. Because the job description comprises the employee's contract with the organization, it serves as a basis for performance evaluation.
3. Request the standards of nursing practice for the specialty from the appropriate professional association.
4. Create stated position requirements that a prospective employee must have in order to be hired.
5. Define the line of accountability. It should be clear to whom, and for what, the employee is accountable.
6. Write a position summary. This consists of a few statements that briefly describe the position's main functions and responsibilities.
7. Complete a list of duties, responsibilities, and tasks. Many times the nursing process is described in format as opposed to specifics.
8. Check to make sure all responsibilities are competency or criteria based. Utilize the format of "does not meet," "meets," or "exceeds" as an evaluation guide.

9. Get feedback from staff members and the personnel department. Staff can evaluate how clearly responsibilities are communicated. The personnel department can evaluate the legal and institutional issues in regard to these responsibilities.

Table 2-1 compares nurse practice act legislation and a medical center's job description for a registered nurse, a licensed practical nurse, and a nurse aide. Table 2-2 is a more detailed outline comparing the functions and tasks of each group. Remember, these are only examples. Before designing job descriptions for their own institutions, nurse managers should check their own state's nurse practice act along with their individual organization's policies and procedures.

Effective Delegation

For delegation to be effective, the person delegating must provide clear instructions, actively guide the person doing the task, and be involved

Table 2-1.   Comparison of Nurse Practice Act and Institutional Job Description

	Registered Nurse	Licensed Practical Nurse	Nurse Aide
Nurse Practice Act	"The Practice of Professional Nursing means diagnosing and treating human responses to actual or potential health problems through such services as case finding, health teaching, health counseling, and provision of care supporting or restoring life and well-being and executing medical regimens as prescribed by a licensed physician or dentist."	"The performance of selected nursing acts in the care of the ill, injured, infirm under the direction of a licensed professional nurse, a licensed physician or licensed dentist that do not require the specialized skill, judgment, and knowledge required in professional nursing."	None
Institutional job description	Responsible to the nurse manager or clinical head nurse for assessing, planning, implementing, and evaluating nursing care to a designated group of patients.	Responsible to the RN for the performance of various nursing functions pertaining to patient care, treatment, and rehabilitation.	Directly responsible to RN for performing basic bedside care and selected nursing procedures.

Adapted with permission from Department of Nursing, Penn State University Hospital, The Milton S. Hershey Medical Center, Theresa A. (Martini) Herb, M. Ed., R.N., 1989.

Table 2-2.   The Roles and Tasks of Registered Nurses, Licensed Practical Nurses, and Nurse Aides

Roles and Functions		
Registered Nurse	**Licensed Practical Nurse**	**Nurse Aide**
• Manages patient care; accountable for patient care outcome		
• Makes rounds on all patients; performs head-to-toe assessment; plans care		
• Prescribes nursing care needed for patients		
• Makes rounds with attending physician		
• Determines treatment plan, outcome, and compliance with DRG length of stay		
• Delegates tasks to associates, making appropriate assignments		
• Uses clinical judgment and integrates data to predict patient outcome		
• Determines nursing orders		
• Uses critical thinking in making decisions		
• Evaluates care given by coworkers		
• Communicates frequently with coworkers		
• Knows coworkers' abilities and knowledge		
• Gives shift report on all patients	• Listens to the change-of-shift report and contributes to the end-of-shift report	• Listens to the change-of-shift report
• Plans patient teaching and documents	• Reinforces instructions and teaching given by an RN	
• Admits patients and writes assessment notes	• Escorts/orients patients to room and informs RN	• Escorts/orients patients to room and informs RN
• Discharges patients and writes discharge notes	• Takes vital signs, height and weight	• Takes vital signs, height and weight
• Performs nursing research		• Transports patient to door

(continued on next page)

Table 2-2. (Continued)

Tasks		
Registered Nurse	**Licensed Practical Nurse**	**Nurse Aide**
• Provides direct nursing care to select patients and oversees nursing care of all patients—unstable/complex	• Provides direct nursing care to patients under supervision of RN	• Provides direct nursing care under supervision of RN
—Administers IV medications	—Administers PO/IM/NG medications	
	—Maintains patient's daily hygiene	—Maintains patient's daily hygiene
	—Answers call lights	—Answers call lights
	—Administers treatments	—Administers treatments
	—Prepares and changes sterile dressings	
	—Prepares patients for medications and assists with feedings	—Prepares patients for medications and assists with feedings
	—Provides patients with fresh water	—Provides patients with fresh water
	—Maintains bedside medical record	—Documents the bedside medical record
	—Offers and empties bedpans/urinals	—Offers and empties bedpans/urinals
	—Administers enemas	—Administers enemas
	—Monitors vital signs	—Monitors vital signs
	—Applies hot/cold compresses	—Applies hot/cold compresses
	—Applies protection devices	—Applies protection devices
	—Applies elastic stockings	—Applies elastic stockings
	—Prepares and changes nonsterile dressings	—Prepares and changes nonsterile dressings
	—Makes beds	—Makes beds
	—Administers sitz baths	—Administers sitz baths
	—Weighs patients and determines height	—Weighs patients and determines height
	—Collects specimens (routine urine, clean-catch urine, 24-hour urine, urine specific gravity, stool collection, hematest stool)	—Collects specimens (routine urine, clean-catch urine, 24-hour urine, urine specific gravity, stool collection, hematest stool)

Table 2-2. (Continued)

Tasks *(continued)*		
Registered Nurse	**Licensed Practical Nurse**	**Nurse Aide**
	—Assists physician with physical exam	—Assists physician with physical exam
	—Provides postmortem care	—Provides postmortem care
	—Uses glucometer	
	—Observes and records in medical record symptoms and variations in patient condition and reports to RN accountable for patient's care	—Reports changes to RN accountable for patient's care

Adapted, with permission, from Department of Nursing, Penn State University Hospital, The Milton S. Hershey Medical Center, Theresa A. (Martini) Herb, M.Ed., R.N., 1989.

in tracking results and evaluating performance. The eight steps to effective delegation are as follows:

1. Define the task.
   - Identify the duties you perform that could be reasonably delegated.
   - Delegate the whole task whenever possible. Try not to divide one task up for different people, but whenever it is feasible, allow one person to handle the entire task.
   - Avoid gaps (for example, between shifts) and overlaps (for example, having two people pursue the same information for different projects or reasons).
2. Enroll the competent person.
   - Select the individual by matching his or her qualifications with the requirements of the task or assignment.
   - Beware of overdelegating (for example, giving a clinically difficult patient to a novice nurse) or underdelegating (for example, not allowing the neophyte nurse to participate in providing care with supervision).
   - Be reasonable. Make sure the person you select has the time available to handle the delegated task.
3. Lead and empower.
   - Give clear instructions.
   - Make the nonverbal instructions congruent to the verbal (for example, delegate in an assertive rather than apologetic manner).
   - Delegate for specific results.

4. Establish deadlines.
   - Agree on a schedule.
   - Follow up as deadlines arrive.
5. Grant the appropriate level of authority after evaluating the situation and the individual. (The next subsection describes this step in more detail.)
6. Guide the person actively.
   - Share ideas, beliefs, feelings, and anticipated problems.
   - Provide necessary direction.
   - Be willing to negotiate.
   - Reach an agreement.
7. Track for results.
   - Identify the information or feedback you will need in order to stay informed and maintain overall control (written reports or brief oral reports, for example).
   - Do not complete an assignment for a coworker. If the individual to whom you have delegated an assignment has failed to complete it, hold him or her accountable.
   - Identify critical events or milestones that should be brought to your attention.
   - Think about potential problems that may arise and discuss how they might be resolved by the coworker.
8. Evaluate performance.
   - Measure how well the individual has achieved the described results (for example, quality of work, timeliness). Also note any improvement in the individual's performance.
   - Evaluate how well he or she stayed within the boundaries of the delegated authority.

Delegate Appropriate Levels of Authority

Delegating is not an all-or-nothing process. Obviously, employees who are new to the job cannot assume the same amount of responsibility as veteran employees. By incorporating a concept known as *levels of authority,* nurse managers can decide the level of responsibility and authority an individual can assume. The following four levels of delegated authority are progressive in nature:

- Level I: Do only what I tell you to do.
  - This is what I want you to do. (Be specific.)
  - Report the facts of a problem to me.
  - I'll decide what to do.
- Level II: Get approval before moving on.
  - Look into the problem.

−Let me know what you intend to do.
−Do not take action until I approve.
* Level III: Report the problem-solving action taken.
−Take action.
−Let me know what you did.
* Level IV: Report back only if there is an unresolved problem.
−Take action.
−Contact me only if there is a problem.

The following example illustrates how the four levels of authority might work:

> *Mr. Smith is a three-day postcoronary bypass patient. He has progressed slowly and suffered more than the usual amount of pain. His wife has frequently spoken to the nurse manager and physician about her fear that her husband will die. Yesterday, it took 15 minutes for Mr. Smith to receive his pain medication. Distressed about the wait, Mrs. Smith called the patient representative and the physician, Dr. Houston. Now the wife has complained again about her husband's care on the evening shift. She has phoned Dr. Houston and threatened to call the president of the hospital. The nurse manager delegates authority for resolving this problem in one of the following ways:*

* Level I: "Check with your coworkers and Mr. Smith to find out what the problem is concerning his satisfaction with his care. Please let me know what you find by 2:00 p.m. I'll talk to Dr. Houston and Mrs. Smith when they come this afternoon."

* Level II: "Please look into the problem. Tell me what actions you think you and your coworkers need to take and why. Recommend one to me by 2:00 p.m. We will then discuss what the appropriate action should be."

* Level III: "Let me know what action you take with the family and what you said to Dr. Houston."

* Level IV: "Let me know if you are unable to resolve the problem. Otherwise, I will assume it is taken care of."

Three factors need to be considered when deciding which level of authority to give a particular nurse:

1. Competency of the nurse
   * Skill level in problem solving
   * Ability to deal with conflict situations

2. Impact of the decision
   - Ability to understand and appropriately handle politically sensitive issues
   - Knowledge of effects on other departments
3. Type of information needed to perform the delegated activity
   - Some confidential information that cannot be divulged

As noted, there may be some limitations on what can be delegated. For example, a new nurse might not understand the politically sensitive nature of managing a board member who is demanding that his or her room be changed or that he or she be allowed to do something against hospital policy. As another example, a patient may have revealed some delicate information to the nurse manager about discharge plans, and sharing this information with the staff nurse would be breaching the patient's confidentiality. In these cases, delegation would not be advisable.

Nurses and other health care workers usually progress from level I to level IV the longer their tenure on the unit. As nurse managers build trust in individuals' competencies, they gradually delegate more to these individuals.

Assess the Outcomes of the Delegation

In evaluating the outcomes of delegation, three questions must be answered to determine whether positive recognition, coaching, or counseling is the appropriate response to the subordinate's performance:

1. Did he or she achieve the desired results?
   - Was the task completed with the expected outcome?
   - Was the task completed on time?
2. Has his or her performance improved?
   - Compared with the previous task, has he or she made progress in efficiency and/or effectiveness?
3. Did he or she stay within the bounds of delegated authority?
   - Did he or she use appropriate means to solve the problem or exceed set limits to do so (for example, by contacting someone out of the scope of his or her authority)?
   - Did he or she follow policy and the Nurse Practice Act (which may limit the individual's scope of practice)?

If the answer to all three questions is yes, then positive recognition is warranted. If the answer to any of the questions is no, then nurse managers should coach employees on how to improve performance. The following is an example of coaching:

The staff has been complaining to you that supplies are not available when needed. The inventory/equipment assistant has the responsibility for placing weekly storeroom orders and maintaining par levels. The question is whether the par levels are sufficient and the assistant is placing the appropriate orders. On questioning him, you find that the levels are insufficient. Although he was aware this was a problem, he failed to bring it to your attention. You then coach the assistant by encouraging him to take the initiative in problem solving. You ask him to look into the problem and to let you know what he plans to do by Friday.

Coaching helps assistants take a more empowered approach to their jobs. In the example above, the nurse manager instructs and advises the assistant on how to improve his performance. If the assistant fails to improve performance, the nurse manager may need to implement a more formal counseling process. The following is an example in which initial counseling is used:

The nurse manager calls the assistant into her office and states, "A week and a half ago I asked you to look into the problem of patient supplies and bring your plans of change to me for approval. Supplies continue to be unavailable when needed. In a conversation with Mr. Jenny in Purchasing, I discovered you have not had any discussion with him. It is a week past the time I asked you to present your plan to me. First, I would like to understand why you didn't follow up; and second, I would like to know when I can expect your recommended change in par levels."

Managers are responsible for evaluating the delegated task. Figure 2-1 provides a checklist for the manager to use in determining whether he or she delegated and followed up correctly. If the answers to the questions on the checklist are yes, then the manager delegated effectively. If the answer to any of the questions is no, managers should look into the situation and determine what the problems are.

The next two sections explore some reasons for ineffective delegation and techniques for more effective delegation.

Some Reasons for Ineffective Delegation or Failure to Delegate

Most managers have reasons for not delegating or ineffectively delegating responsibility. Breaking the do-it-yourself habit is more difficult for some than for others. Because nurse managers are hesitant to give up some control or are afraid to admit that they simply do not know how to delegate, the reasons given for not delegating are often rationalizations.

Figure 2-1. Delegation Follow-up Assessment Checklist

YES   NO

____ ____ 1. Did the individual complete the assigned task?

____ ____ 2. Did he/she complete it within the appropriate time frame?

____ ____ 3. Has his/her performance improved since the last time you observed his/her response to this delegation?

____ ____ 4. Have you acknowledged his/her achievement?

____ ____ 5. Have you discussed ways to improve his/her performance?

____ ____ 6. If a problem occurred, did you discuss what he/she would have liked you to do differently and what you would have liked him/her to do differently?

____ ____ 7. In your problem resolution, did you reach an agreement on how to resolve the problem and/or did you take the issue to your director for help in problem resolution?

____ ____ 8. Did you determine whether it is time to give this individual even more responsibility and authority in your next delegation?

Figure 2-2 lists the 15 most common reasons people fail to delegate, beginning with organizational problems and progressing to the manager's own idiosyncrasies.

Following are three typical categories of delegation problems, which include many of the causes listed in figure 2-2:

- Vague organizational directions
- Interference with the empowerment process
- Managers' idiosyncrasies

Any of these can make nurse managers hesitant to delegate.

Vague Organizational Direction

It is difficult for managers to delegate effectively without clear organizational goals and direction. An organization without clear direction often leaves nurse managers guessing as to the most appropriate expenditure of their time. Regardless of the nursing department's lack of strategy, the nurse manager must develop goals with his or her staff that will provide the unit with some focus and direction. Nurse managers must help their staff establish clear standards of nursing practice and levels of nursing competency for the unit. Clinical competence can then be measured against organizational and professional standards. This comparison provides the

Figure 2-2. Fifteen Most Common Causes of Ineffective Delegation

_____ 1. Ambiguous organizational objectives that leave you conflicted over priorities

_____ 2. Lack of performance standards or guidelines leading to unclear definition of job responsibilities

_____ 3. Lack of common understanding of the specifics of the task delegated

_____ 4. Lack of proper training for subordinates

_____ 5. Lack of confidence in the subordinates' capabilities

_____ 6. Interference by the superior in the delegated assignment

_____ 7. Interference by superior's superior in the delegated assignment

_____ 8. Fear of criticism

_____ 9. Fear of punitive action by superiors

_____ 10. Lack of self-confidence and unwillingness to take necessary risks

_____ 11. Fear that the subordinate will perform better than the manager would have performed

_____ 12. Strong desire to be liked by subordinates

_____ 13. Reluctance to delegate preferred tasks

_____ 14. Unwillingness to make mistakes or to allow others to make mistakes (insistence on perfection)

_____ 15. Failure to establish adequate follow-up procedures with a delegated assignment

framework for identifying staff development needs and quality assurance issues. Once these mechanisms are in place, the nurse manager can then begin to delegate responsibilities that are in line with the established goals and standards.

Interference with the Empowerment Process

Delegation problems may also be caused by supervisors who fail to understand the concept of empowerment. They hold the management reins too tightly or interfere with the nurse manager's delegation. Nurse managers will need to determine their supervisors' concerns and provide appropriate detail and follow-up information to help them feel comfortable in exerting less control.

Managers' Idiosyncrasies

More frequently, the nurse manager's idiosyncrasies prevent appropriate delegation. Unwillingness to take the necessary risks may be caused by perfectionism. It is hard for nurse managers to remember that often they are successful despite, not because of, their perfectionism. Because the work of others rarely meets their excessively high standards, perfectionists tend to be poor delegators. They would rather do it themselves and have it done "right" than accept the employees' work that often adequately meets the institution's, if not the nurse manager's, standards.

Furthermore, the constantly critical attitude of the perfectionist nurse manager takes a toll on staff members' self-esteem. When perfectionism is compounded by a desire to be liked and a reluctance to delegate preferred tasks, the end result is a nurse manager who works 12 or more hours a day and fails to experience the satisfaction that comes from being a mentor.

Two statements indicative of the manager who fails to delegate sufficiently are:

- "My staff is already overwhelmed with work. How can I delegate more?"
- "I'm the one who gets the criticism if they fail to do the job."

However, it is possible for nurse managers to overcome the feelings inherent in these statements. By delegating effectively, as well as subsequently training staff to delegate some of their work to others, all employee time is used more efficiently and effectively.

The issue of receiving criticism from superiors surfaces for nurse managers when they fail to maintain an adequate delegation follow-up system. As suggested earlier, instructing employees effectively during delegation will help them assume accountability. Nurse managers need to gradually relinquish authority as they continually monitor each individual's ability to take responsibility.

How to Increase Positive Responses to Delegation

Thirteen suggestions on how to increase the likelihood of a positive response by a subordinate to a delegated task are as follows:

1. Explain the "why" of the assignment. Give reasons for your delegation.
2. Be willing to give the staff member the necessary authority.
3. Make sure the details of the task are clear to you so that you can explain them to the staff member.
4. Adapt all details and instructions to the staff member's knowledge and level of understanding.
5. Give assignments, in addition to their routine tasks, that provide challenging opportunities to staff members.

6. Provide ongoing training to help staff members keep up their skills.
7. Put instructions in writing if the procedure is complicated.
8. Do not give assignments and then take them away before the staff member develops competence in the delegated task (for example, developing scheduling and staffing assignments).
9. Evaluate continually your level of control taking (for example, you may be following up sooner than is necessary).
10. Delegate the whole task whenever possible.
11. Reprimand mistakes in private, focusing on resolution of the problem.
12. Give praise to staff members who do the job well.
13. Focus your energy on achieving higher level skills for yourself as you delegate to staff members.

Delegation enables nurse managers to build a high-performance team by maximizing the use of all members' skill levels. By delegating, the nurse manager also fosters staff empowerment and professional development. However, conflicts are inevitable when the roles people play change. Nurses often speak of encountering conflict when they begin to practice delegation. As they hold individuals accountable for their practice, interpersonal conflicts arise. The skills discussed in the following section on conflict resolution are vitally important in the management process.

☐ Conflict Resolution

Conflict is a clash or disagreement in individuals' ideas or interests. As nurse managers become leaders and coaches, they will frequently engage in conflict with staff members who have different ideas of management's role. Delegation of certain responsibilities formerly assumed to be those of management can also lead to role conflict.

Conflict is recognized as a natural part of resolving divergent opinions. Resolving conflict is crucial in the health care environment because of health care providers' interdependent roles.

As noted, role changes create uncertainty among workers and predispose them to conflict. However, conflict is constructive when it (1) opens up issues of importance, resulting in solutions to problems; (2) serves as a release for pent-up emotions; and (3) helps individuals grow personally and apply what they have learned to future situations.[3] When the nurse manager facilitates conflict resolution, the team becomes more cohesive. Because nurse managers serve as role models for staff members, it is crucial that the nurse managers learn and practice conflict resolution skills.

Conflicts arise in any change process because change brings an individual's basic assumptions into question. Most people have preconceived ideas of right and wrong and what actions are or are not appropriate. A change in roles tests these ideas. Some individuals cling to their definition of the way it should be and battle to maintain their "right" point of view. Other individuals stand up for their beliefs and engage in a dialogue to reach a negotiated solution. The remainder of this chapter focuses on how to do the latter and how to teach staff to effectively manage change.

There are five conflict resolution strategies:

- Avoid the conflict
- Win–lose
- Preserve the relationship
- Compromise
- Win–win

The most effective strategy is win–win because both parties come away feeling they have gained rather than lost. The second most desirable is compromise. Sometimes compromise is the only choice when a win–win strategy cannot be realized with someone who is using a win–lose strategy. In those situations, the best that can be hoped for is a compromise.

A discussion of the five conflict resolution strategies follows. Examples are given for when it is appropriate or inappropriate to use each strategy.

Avoid the Conflict

People who withdraw to avoid conflict give up their personal goals and often fail to form effective interpersonal relationships. They stay away from defining the issues in the conflict and from the people involved. They believe it is hopeless or useless to try to resolve conflicts and find it easier to withdraw (physically and psychologically) from conflict than to face it. They use avoidance not out of choice, but out of fear.

However, avoidance can be used appropriately when an individual decides to withdraw temporarily. Appropriate temporary withdrawal occurs primarily in two situations:

- When one of the individuals involved in the conflict is out of control and any attempt toward resolution could cause further escalation of inappropriate behavior
- When responding to conflict in the situation would be socially inappropriate

Win–Lose

People who use the win–lose strategy assume that conflicts are settled by one person winning and the other losing, and they want to be the winner. Winning gives them a sense of pride and achievement; losing gives them a sense of weakness, inadequacy, and failure. They try to win by attacking, overpowering, overwhelming, and intimidating others. People who try to overpower opponents by forcing them to accept their goals or solutions often view interpersonal relationship as having minor importance. Because they seek to achieve their goals at all costs, they are not concerned with the needs of others. They do not care if other people like or accept them.

However, it is appropriate and reasonable to use a win–lose approach when an issue is not negotiable—when legal, ethical, or moral issues are at stake. For instance, when the safety and quality of care are threatened, a nurse manager may need to choose a win–lose strategy.

Preserve the Relationship

For some other people, maintaining interpersonal relationships is of greater importance than achieving their own goals. They want to be accepted and liked. They believe conflict should be avoided in favor of harmony and that conflicts cannot be discussed without damaging relationships. They are afraid that if the conflict continues, someone will be hurt, and a relationship will be ruined. They give up their goals to preserve the relationship, saying, in effect, "I'll give up my goals and let you have what you want so that you will like me."

On the other hand, when the outcome lacks importance or relevance to an individual, it may be better to go along with the other's goals. For example, the staff nurses might insist that holiday coverage be the first topic on the agenda for a staff meeting. If the nurse manager has no key issue with a higher priority, then the manager should change the agenda accordingly. In addition, if unable to reach a win–win or a compromise solution and the issue is not important, the nurse manager may choose to preserve the relationship. At other times, it also may be politically sensitive to give in on one issue, with the long-term goal of winning more important battles down the line. The important difference here is that nurse managers *choose* to give in; they do not abdicate responsibility.

Compromise

When individuals are moderately concerned with their own goals and their relationships with other people, they seek to compromise. They seek a solution in which both sides gain something, taking the middle ground between two extreme positions. Compromisers are willing to sacrifice some of their goals and risk hurting relationships for the common good.

A compromise is appropriate when a win–win solution cannot be reached, either because the person sees his or her relationship with the other party as unimportant or because they present their goals as inflexible. For example, a nurse manager wants to change the flow sheets to include five more sources of data. Staff members want only three, perceiving the other two as unnecessary. Possible compromises include reducing the number of data sources to four or using additional sources of data for three months on a trial basis.

Win–Win

The win–win strategy is a problem-solving approach in which both individuals seek to have their goals met. When people value their goals and their relationships highly, they view conflicts as problems to be solved. They seek solutions that achieve both their own goals and those of the others involved in the conflict. These individuals see conflicts as opportunities to improve relationships by reducing tensions between people. They are not satisfied until a solution is found that achieves their own and the other person's goals or until the tension and negative feelings have been fully resolved. For example, a staff nurse may request a weekend off that the nurse manager cannot grant. The win–win solution comes as a result of negotiation. They determine that Saturday is the crucial part of the weekend needed by the staff nurse, and the nurse manager can grant her that day off.

Conflict resolution requires both assertiveness and negotiation skills as described in the following two sections. To effectively resolve conflict, it is especially important for nurse managers who use the win–win or compromise techniques to develop these key skills.

☐ Assertiveness

Assertive behavior is a type of interpersonal behavior in which individuals stand up for their legitimate rights in a way that does not violate the rights of others. Assertive behavior is an honest, direct, and appropriate expression of one's feelings, thoughts, and opinions. Such behavior communicates respect for the other person, although not necessarily for that person's behavior.

The description of a person as "too assertive" is a misnomer. Either the individual describing the situation feels threatened, or the assertive person is actually acting in an aggressive manner.

Aggressive behavior exists when individuals attempt to humiliate, dominate, or put down other people rather than to simply express honest feelings or thoughts. Assertive nurse managers speak directly to staff members, stating issues honestly, as they see them, and choosing an appropriate place for interactions (not in front of others, for example). They not only express their own ideas, opinions and feelings in regard to issues, they encourage others to do so as well.

Key Situations for Demonstrating Assertive Behavior

There are four situations in which assertive behavior should be practiced:

- When expressing positive feelings
- When expressing negative feelings
- When setting limits
- When asking for what one wants

The first two situations focus on expressing feelings; the second two on expressing wants. Most individuals have trouble asserting themselves in various situations. Nurse managers should assess their own strengths and weaknesses when utilizing assertive behavior in these four types of situations. Examples of each type of situation are as follows:

1. Expressing positive feelings:
   - "I like you."
   - "You did a good job teaching ostomy care to Mr. Jones."
   - "You are demonstrating a good grasp of setting priorities early in your orientation."
2. Expressing negative feelings:
   - "I don't like it when you continually interrupt me."
   - "I feel disappointed that you didn't keep our agreement."
   - "I feel angry when you come to staff meetings late and then ask to be updated on what was said."
3. Setting limits:
   - "No, I am not willing to grant your attendance at an educational program in Honolulu."
   - "I would like you to knock before you walk into my office."
   - "I want you to submit your requests for time off according to policy."
4. Asking for what you want:
   - "I would like you to ask the Nurse Practice Council to determine a way to assign patients to primary nurses who do not volunteer to take patients."
   - "I want you to resolve the conflict with Susan; if you can't, then come to me."
   - "I would like you to think through your problem and come to me not just with problems, but with options to solve them."

Assertiveness can be expressed both verbally and nonverbally. The following subsections discuss both verbal and nonverbal assertiveness. Strategies for dealing with negative responses to assertive behavior will also be discussed.

Verbal Assertiveness

The verbal component of assertive behavior is best depicted in "I" statements, describing what is wanted and using objective words that say what is meant. The verbal component of nonassertive behavior contains apologetic words, may appear rambling, and sometimes includes the phrase "you know." Aggressive verbal behavior is filled with accusations, subjective words, and "you" messages that blame or label.

An assertive message contains the following four components:

1. A nonjudgmental description of the behavior to be changed
2. A disclosure of honest feelings
3. An explanation of the concrete and tangible effect of the other person's behavior
4. A statement of the solution desired or an invitation to solve the problem

The formula for using these components is as follows:

When you _____1_____, I feel _____2_____
because _____3_____. I'd like _____4_____.

Following are three examples using this formula:

- "When you come to work 20 minutes late without notifying me, I feel frustrated because I spent the time arranging for other coverage. I'd like you to call if you are going to be late."
- "When you go to lunch and make no arrangements to have someone cover your patients, I feel concerned because it affects safety and quality of care in this unit. I'd like you to make sure you arrange coverage."
- "When you tell me something you say is confidential and I then hear you telling a whole group the same thing in the nurses' lounge, I feel confused because the behavior is inconsistent, and I therefore question your judgment. I'd like to understand this discrepancy."

All these phrases clearly state the behavior nurse managers want changed, their feelings, the consequences of the behavior, and a request for change or clarification.

Nonverbal Assertiveness

Many assertive statements can be perceived as aggressive or nonassertive depending on the nonverbal behavior that accompanies them. Table 2-3 describes the nonverbal components of nonassertive, assertive, and aggressive behavior. The four factors of nonverbal behavior are: voice, eyes, stance/posture, and hands. For example, if the nurse manager delivers an assertive statement such as, "When you repeatedly ask me the same question about Mr. Jones's discharge planning, I feel confused because I don't know if I'm not explaining it clearly or if you are not listening. I'd like to know what you have heard me say about his discharge plans."

If the nurse manager uses a superior voice and points her finger, the individual will experience aggression, not a statement designed for clearing up communication.

It is important to remember that when incongruent verbal and nonverbal messages are sent, people will unconsciously believe the nonverbal message. An incongruent message is confusing. Therefore, congruent verbal and nonverbal statements carry the most potent message.

Table 2-3.   Nonverbal Components of Behaviors

Components	Nonassertive	Assertive	Aggressive
A. General	Hoping someone will guess what you want; looking as if you don't mean what you say	Attentive listening behavior; general assured manner, communicating caring and strength	Flippant, sarcastic style; air of superiority
B. Specific			
1. Voice	Weak, hesitant, soft, sometimes wavering	Firm, well-modulated, relaxed	Tense, shrill, loud, shaky, cold, demanding, superior, authoritarian
2. Eyes	Averted, downcast, teary, pleading	Open, frank, direct	Expressionless, cold, staring, not really "seeing" others
3. Stance/ Posture	Leaning for support, stooped, excessive head nodding	Well-balanced, feet slightly apart, erect, relaxed	Hands on hips, stiff and rigid, imperious
4. Hands	Fidgety, fluttery, clammy	Relaxed motions	Clenched, abrupt gestures, finger pointing, fist pounding

Source: Based on Bolton, R. *People Skills*. Englewood Cliffs, New Jersey: Prentice-Hall, 1979.

Positive Responses to Assertive Behavior

A positive response to an assertive statement focuses on problem solving, not on defensiveness or overadaptation. For example, a positive response to the statement, "When you repeatedly ask me the same question about Mr. Jones's discharge planning, I feel confused because I don't know if I'm not explaining it clearly or if you are not listening. I'd like to know what you have heard me say about his discharge plans," could be either of the following:

- "I'm sorry I'm not paying attention to your explanation. Let me tell you what I understood you to say."
- "This is the first time I've dealt with a discharge to a hospital in another state. I guess I feel unsure of what I'm doing."

Negative Responses to Assertive Behavior

Not all situations result in a positive response. The following subsections explore negative responses and focus on techniques to cope with them.

Defensive Behavior

When individuals actively repel an actual or perceived attack, they are acting defensively. If, in fact, individuals are in a dangerous position, then protecting themselves from harm is an appropriate response. However, in most cases, individuals are not actually in danger, but are responding out of fear.

It is important to remember that underneath an angry veneer lies a scared little boy or girl. In fact, the louder the bark and the greater the overreaction, the more the person is avoiding dealing with his or her underlying fear. Many people are unable to admit their fears and that they feel out of control in dealing with certain situations. Therefore, they use hostile, intimidating behavior in an effort to force others to do as they wish.

In such tense situations, it is difficult to focus on a person's emotions as well as the facts. However, to do so is the key to coping with angry, defensive people. Because most people respond defensively to hostility, focusing on solving the problem will defuse emotions and eventually the person will stop trying to exert control.

There are two strategies for handling a defensive response: (1) reflecting the other person's argument and (2) clarifying the interaction. Reflecting the other person's argument means first focusing on what is agreed with and disagreed with in the other party's verbal and nonverbal communication. It is important to focus on the other person's content and feelings, with a special emphasis on feelings. For example, "Dr. Houston, you have every right to be upset that your patient got the wrong medication. However, screaming at Mr. Smith's nurse in front of him is unacceptable."

A second possible response to defensive behavior is for the nurse manager to clarify the interaction by asking, "What did you hear me say?" If the person responds with an accurate restatement of what was said, then the response can be, "When you respond so angrily to my statement, I feel confused because I want only to solve the problem." If the person responds differently, the nurse manager might say, "What I wanted you to hear me say was . . ." and repeat the assertive statement. Here is an example of how such a dialogue might sound:

Nurse Manager: "When you go to lunch and make no arrangements to have someone cover your patients, I feel concerned, because it affects the safety and quality of care in this unit. I would like you to make sure you arrange coverage."

Staff Nurse: (with anger) "I'm a good nurse."

Nurse Manager: "What did you hear me say?"

Staff Nurse: "You said that I was not caring for my patients."

Nurse Manager: "What I wanted you to hear me say is that I am asking you to arrange for coverage for your patients before you leave the unit."

It should be noted that in these examples, *but* is not used. Linguistically, *but* eradicates the first part of the sentence. Using *and* says to the person that a positive and a negative can exist simultaneously. This is important to remember, especially when dealing with people who have low self-esteem. When hearing negative comments, these individuals forget their positive attributes and begin to defend the little self-esteem they do have. People with positive self-esteem are more likely to accept negative feedback, because they are able to keep it in perspective.

Hostile Behavior

The extremely hostile person is often referred to as a "Sherman tank." Typical behaviors seen in people who choose this type of approach include the following:

- They are abusive, abrupt, intimidating, overwhelming, and arrogant.
- They attack in an accusing way.
- They try to prove they are right.
- They become impatient with those who do not see their point.

- They become irritated when they experience resistance.
- They express a strong opinion regarding what others "should" do.

The following eight processes can be used when coping with extremely hostile individuals:

1. Stand up for yourself. Expect to feel awkward, fearful, or confused. Stand up anyway.
2. Give them time to run down.
3. When the momentum dies down, get their attention by calling them by name. With a sharp inflection or enough volume to break through, repeatedly say, "Stop, stop" or "Wait a minute." For example, "Dr. Smith, stop, wait a minute."
4. If possible, get them to sit down. People behave less aggressively when seated. Interrupt the hostile interaction by moving to another room.
5. Speak from your own point of view in a normal tone of voice, starting with what you agree with and moving to what you disagree with in their statement. For example, "I agree with you . . . and I disagree with you. . . ." Use as few words as possible.
6. Repeat the preceding as often as necessary to keep the discussion focused on the problem.
7. Avoid a head-on fight. The behavior is likely to escalate, and such people tend to be good at fighting. If defeated, the aggressor may go "underground" and use passive-aggressive behavior.
8. Stand up for yourself and gain the person's respect.

Here is an example of a nurse manager dealing with a Sherman tank: "I agree. Mr. Smith's nurse should have known the medication was not appropriate for him. I disagree with the idea that her mistake gives you the right to belittle her in front of the patient."

Passive-Aggressive Behavior

Sherman tanks can become snipers; that is, individuals who demonstrate passive-aggressive behavior. They may take pot shots, give not too subtle criticisms, talk about someone behind their back, or tease nonplayfully.

The best way to cope with a sniper is to bring the attack to the surface with such statements as, "That sounded like a dig. Did you mean it that way?" Or "What did you mean when you turned your thumbs down while I was telling my story?" All responses should be phrased as questions rather than assertions.

If the sniper continues with something like "Oh, you are so sensitive" or indicates in some way that the manager is overreacting to a pot shot, the same question can be repeated. In assertiveness training, such repetition is called the *broken record technique.* It can be used when individuals try to change the subject or when the situation is nonnegotiable. The following is an example of a dialogue in which a nurse manager confronts a staff nurse using the broken record technique. The staff nurse has chosen to talk about the nurse manager behind her back rather than speak honestly and directly with her about a disagreement.

Nurse Manager: "I understand via the grapevine that you were unhappy with the way in which I facilitated the staff meeting yesterday."

Staff Nurse: "Who said it? Who told you that?"

Nurse Manager: "I have encouraged the person to tell you directly about their concern. Right now, I am interested in encouraging you to come to me directly when you disagree with my way of doing things."

Staff Nurse: "I didn't say anything. I don't know what you're talking about."

Nurse Manager: "I want you to know that if you have something negative to say, I would prefer that you speak to me directly."

Staff Nurse: "I don't know what you're talking about."

Nurse Manager: "I just want you to know that if you disagree with me, I would prefer that you came to me directly."

Crying

When an individual responds with tears, the nurse manager needs to reflect and affirm his or her desire to solve the problem. For example, the statement that follows indicates that the nurse manager recognizes the person is upset and invites them to help solve the problem. "I can see that you are upset by what I have said. I'd like to continue to solve the problem. Are you willing to do that?" If the person answers no, then the discussion can be continued another time. If the person says yes, the nurse manager should clarify his or her point further, because he or she is dealing with an individual who is upset.

Withdrawal

When an individual responds with withdrawal, he or she retreats from communicating about the problem. The most common response to individuals who withdraw is to continue to talk to them. However, this may not be the best strategy. Instead, the nurse manager should be silent, observe the other party's body language, and then reassert the desire to solve the problem. If the person continues to be silent, then the nurse manager should say, "I take your silence to mean that you don't want to talk about this and that you will meet my needs by [doing what behavior change is requested]." Sometimes even this will not entice the individual to discuss the issue. The nurse manager should always end with an invitation for the individual to come back and talk at any point in the future and state that the door is always open to discuss the issue.

Confrontational Techniques for Responding to Negative Reactions

Confrontation is often seen as antagonistic communication. However, confrontation can also mean simply a face-to-face meeting. To confront someone is to bring them face-to-face with a problem. There are two confrontation methods for a nurse manager to keep in mind when dealing with negative responses: *negative inquiry* and *awareness raising.*

Negative inquiry forces the receiver of the communication to investigate or examine his or her negative reaction. The nurse manager applies the idea of negative inquiry by examining the negative statement in order to begin the problem-solving process. For example, a staff member has just complained about his or her schedule, and the nurse manager is now about to respond.

Staff Nurse: "This is the worst schedule I've ever had. I thought things would change when we adopted a staffing and scheduling committee, but obviously not."
Nurse Manager: "Specifically, what would you like to see different?"

Awareness raising focuses on helping others see their verbal or nonverbal communication patterns. All of us develop bad communication habits that we do not notice after awhile. Other people can reinforce our bad habits by not saying anything. Sometimes it is best for the nurse manager to begin a conversation with a question, especially if the person may not be aware that his or her performance or communication is problematic. The following two examples of confrontation use the phrase, "Are you aware . . . ":

- "Are you aware that you are interrupting me each time I attempt to answer your question about changing your schedule?"
- "Are you aware that I have made five requests of you to work overtime in the last month, and you have said 'no' each time?"

If the person responds no, the next step is problem solving. If the person says yes, the consequences must be stated. A response to the last example could be the following:

My expectation is that all staff will share in the overtime. We need to fill vacant spots until Mary and Sue return to work next month. The rest of the staff has participated. I'd like to know when I can count on you to help fill the remaining six holes in the schedule.

Conflict Resolution among Staff Members

Nurse managers also need techniques to help staff members resolve conflicts among themselves. One of these techniques is based on Rogers's Rule, named after the psychotherapist Dr. Carl Rogers. Rogers's Rule is useful in helping staff members examine problems and reach win–win solutions in a nondefensive way. This process calls for each person to speak for him or herself only after first accurately restating the ideas and feelings of the previous speaker to that speaker's satisfaction.

Because everyone has to paraphrase what they have heard, they are forced to listen. Often in such situations, individuals simply pretend to listen—either sitting quietly planning what they intend to say or interrupting with their point of view. By using Rogers's Rule, each person begins to see the other person's side, and all work positively toward a common solution.

By using this technique, the nurse manager and his or her staff help to dissolve previous assumptions, understand personality clashes, and reach compromises on previously contested issues. The nurse manager should act as a facilitator and focus on helping both parties to:

- Make clear statements and paraphrases of the issues
- Make clear statements and paraphrases of the proposed solution
- Understand why the conflict occurred and ways to prevent future conflicts
- Understand the agreed-upon solution

As discussed, assertiveness is a key skill in resolving problems and conflicts that may arise in delegation. When nurse managers delegate responsibilities and discover, during follow-up, that individuals have not completed assignments, managers will need to practice direct communication to resolve problems. Managers must be able to deal effectively with negative responses. However, when both individuals act assertively, then negotiation skills are needed to arrive at a win–win solution.

☐ Negotiation

Negotiation is a give-and-take discussion that requires nurse managers to express their ideas assertively. More specifically, negotiation occurs when two or more parties with common and conflicting interests come together to discuss explicit proposals for the purpose of reaching an agreement.[4] Negotiation is collaborative problem solving. It is a process, not an event. In a successful negotiation, one party finds out what the other wants and shows them a way to get it while at the same time getting what they want. This section focuses on the key characteristics, variables, and strategies of successful negotiation.

Characteristics of Successful Negotiators

In order to successfully negotiate a win–win solution to a problem, it is helpful to know what characteristics expert negotiators possess. Six traits of individuals known to be successful negotiators include the following:[5]

- *Planning skills:* Successful negotiators do their homework by first collecting information and then developing a working strategy. Successful negotiators know what outcome they want at the end of the negotiation and always have a bottom line in mind when they enter a negotiation.
- *Ability to think clearly under stress:* Clear thinking can occur only when a negotiator's ego is not involved. When their sense of self-esteem is tied to the outcome of a negotiation, negotiators put their egos in a precarious position. The desire to win is different from the need to win in order to feel good.
- *Ability to use common sense:* Common sense involves an understanding of human behavior and a willingness to establish rapport with other individuals prior to, as well as during, negotiations. If the other individuals believe that the negotiator genuinely cares, they are more open to possibilities presented during the negotiation.
- *Ability to listen to others and articulate one's own needs clearly:* Assertiveness and the ability to listen are equal partners in the negotiation process. To understand others' wants and needs, listening is required. Successful negotiators articulate their needs clearly so that the other party can understand. Clear communication involves speaking distinctively and pronouncing words clearly in well-formulated sentences.
- *Personal integrity:* Successful negotiators know that trust is the foundation for any win–win solution. Trust requires honesty.
- *Ability to perceive and use power:* Successful negotiators are not afraid to take shrewdly calculated risks based on accurate information.

Crucial Variables in Negotiation

In any negotiation, there are three interrelated variables: information, time, and power.[6]

Information

The information a nurse manager has, or lacks, affects his or her appraisal of reality and the decisions he or she makes. Often, managers fail to obtain adequate information, because they tend to regard negotiation encounters as a limited, rather than an ongoing, process. Managers should ask questions, even when they know the answers, because it tests the credibility of the other side. It is important for managers to listen for cues or messages that are sent indirectly. These messages can be unintentional, such as a Freudian slip. They can also be behavioral, such as body posture, facial expressions, or eye contact. Finally, verbal cues (voice intonation or emphasis, for example) can give important information, especially when such cues contradict the words being spoken. Understanding what the other party needs is crucial to a win–win negotiation.

Time

Patience is the most important aspect of managing negotiation time. In any negotiation, the most significant concession behavior and any settlement action usually occur close to the deadline. For example, in negotiating overtime work with a staff nurse at 9:00 a.m. or at 2:00 p.m, an effective manager quickly sees who has the advantage in negotiation at 2:00 p.m.

Power

Power is the capacity or ability to get things done. The nurse manager has many sources of power, including the following:[7]

- *Power of legitimacy:* Legitimacy can be used, questioned, and challenged when it is advantageous to do so. For example, "I am sorry, Doctor, but that is our policy here," or "I know that is the transfer policy. However, this patient is in no condition to wait for the paperwork."
- *Power of risk taking:* It is important to take moderate or incremental risks—risks the manager can afford without being worried about adverse consequences. It is also important to mix courage with common sense. Whenever possible, the risks should be shared with other individuals. For example, a nurse manager may want the nursing department to pursue a shared governance model. Instead of bringing the idea to nursing administration, she could recruit seven other managers and develop a joint proposal.
- *Power of expertise:* People treat an individual with a consideration that ranges from respect to awe when they perceive that he or she has more knowledge or skills than they have. The manager should avoid appearing

pretentious, but offer his or her expertise by establishing background and credentials. For example, in budget negotiations, it is important to be prepared, to be able to ask intelligent questions, and to know whether one is getting accurate responses.

- *Power of the knowledge of "needs:"* If one can reasonably guess another person's needs, one can predict, with remarkable certainty, what will happen in many interactions.
- *Power of reward or punishment:* One's perception that another individual can help or hurt him or her gives the other person "muscle" in a negotiation. All staff nurses know that nurse managers have the power to reward and punish through their legitimate authority in the organization. For example, a nurse manager can reward the staff nurses who worked diligently on developing teaching tools by agreeing to their request to attend a conference in Orlando. On the other hand, the nurse manager may punish a staff nurse who has not been available for overtime by denying a similar request.
- *Power of identification:* People really are judged by the company they keep. If a nurse manager is seen in the company of powerful people, he or she will be identified as having power.
- *Power of persistence:* Most people are not persistent enough when negotiating. For example, implementing a professional practice model requires persistence as the nurse manager helps staff members acquire the skills necessary for success. Persistent negotiation between staff and management is crucial for such a model's success.
- *Power of persuasion:* Persuasive nurse managers are able to influence the ability of another person to take action or change another's belief by appealing to an individual's reason or emotion. It requires persuasion to convince staff nurses to present care conferences on their patients with rare diseases. A few suggestions for increasing the persuasive impact of various statements are as follows:[8]
  - Present both sides of the issue.
  - Present the desirable message first and the less desirable one second.
  - Present key points at the beginning and the end of the presentation.
  - Tie controversial issues to issues on which agreement can easily be reached.
  - State conclusions explicitly.
  - *Power of attitude:* Caring too much can cost a nurse manager heavily in a negotiation when, in fact, objectivity would pay a higher dividend. If one develops a healthy, somewhat amused, "It's a game" attitude toward negotiations, the experience will be less stressful. The manager is also likely to achieve better results because he or she conveys an impression of mastery.

Key Strategies in Negotiation

Along with the crucial variables of information, time, and power, there are four key strategies in every negotiation:[9]

- *Separate the people from the problem:* The nurse manager will occasionally be in the difficult position of negotiating with people who are unfriendly, hostile, or inflexible or who possess other negative characteristics. In these situations, it is important to attack the problem, not the person. In other words, the nurse manager should be hard on the problems and soft on the people. Negotiation is a problem-solving process. Therefore, the focus should stay on the issue at hand.
- *Focus on interests, not positions:* It is crucial for the nurse manager to focus on interests, not positions, in order to generate options. A position is something that must be decided on; whereas an interest motivates one to choose a position. For example, a nurse manager may have taken the position that only primary nursing can provide the kind of accountability that fosters quality patient care. The other individual sees the case management model as providing better care. Each of these models is an example of a position. When both individuals look for shared and compatible interests, a spirit of reciprocity may emerge.
- *Invent options for mutual gain:* In developing options, brainstorming is often useful. If brainstorming is not used, individuals often stick with tried-and-true solutions. Brainstorming encourages people to leave the either/or options by the wayside. For example, a nurse manager could use brainstorming as a way to generate ideas from staff on how to grant time off at holidays without using seniority as the guideline.
- *Insist on using objective criteria:* It is important to have objective criteria in decision making. For example, if the nurse manager is told to reduce his or her budget by 18 percent, it is appropriate that he or she find out what standards were used to determine that reduction compared to the 12 percent reductions being asked of other units.

In any successful negotiation process, nurse managers must communicate their own interests, they must also seek and acknowledge the interests of others. It is important to look for common goals and develop options for resolving conflicts. During negotiation, it is important for one party to be aware of the other's preferences for solution. When communicating, both parties should listen attentively to the other's feelings. Negotiation involves working out a solution in which both individuals feel satisfied.

Negotiation Exercise

Nurse managers armed with negotiation strategies will begin to notice daily opportunities to practice negotiation skills. These opportunities arise not only with staff, but also with supervisors and peers.

The following paragraphs describe a negotiation situation that may sound familiar. After reading about managers A and B, the reader should take the time to contemplate and answer the questions presented in figure 2-3, answering first from manager A's perspective and then from manager B's perspective.

> *Managers A and B have been given full responsibility by their director for carrying out a major project that will take about six months to complete. This is not the first time these two people have worked together. Two years ago, they worked together on a similar project. The combination of manager A's ability to generate excitement and enthusiasm and manager B's ability to organize and structure tasks resulted in an unusually successful project. They found and shared many similar values and aspirations and came to trust and respect each other's abilities.*
>
> *Manager B has been in her present job for three years and views this project as an opportunity to have a major impact on the direction of the organization. She had decided, therefore, to make this project a number-one personal priority. Manager B is concerned that unless manager A becomes personally involved in the project from the beginning, manager A's subordinates will take their supervisor's behavior as an indication that the project is not of high priority.*
>
> *Manager A has been in her present job for only a few months. She is still busy trying to sort things out and get on top of the new job, especially in the area of staffing the unit. She is spending long hours in formulating clear goals and direction—the key ingredients necessary, from manager A's viewpoint, to generate needed motivation and excitement. This process has turned out to be more difficult and more time-consuming than she had anticipated. Consequently, she has decided to delegate leadership of the new project to a highly competent assistant nurse manager who, although busy, has two years of experience in her current job.*
>
> *Review your answers to the questions in figure 2-3. Were you able to identify the needs and interests of each manager? Manager A needs, along with this project, help in getting on top of her new job, especially in the area of staffing. To impact the organization, manager B needs manager A's personal involvement.*
>
> *Were you able to see options that would satisfy both managers? Manager A might choose to be more involved if manager B helped her with staffing. Perhaps manager A might be involved only in the beginning stages of the project and help to plan and sell ideas to the staff while manager B handles implementation. Can you see a situation that is similar in your work environment and think of ways to apply this process?*

Figure 2-3. Negotiation Exercise

Manager A	Manager B

1. What is the definition of the problem from your perspective?

2. What position is the other manager most likely to take?

3. What are your needs and interests?

4. What are the needs and interests of the manager with whom you are negotiating?

5. What options do you see for a win–win solution?

6. What criteria might you use to evaluate solutions (for example, priorities or time involved)?

7. What could possibly go wrong with your final solutions (for example, can you troubleshoot)?

8. What could you do to prevent or reduce this possible problem?

People no longer accept dictatorial management. The real world is one negotiation after another. Whether the negotiation is about picking Johnny up at day care, establishing time lines for a project, or assigning a staff member to work overtime, agreement is attempted through discussion of issues. Negotiation identifies first what each party wants most and then, second, trades with each other for those needs. Negotiation is a tool for establishing and maintaining trusting, cooperative relationships with staff, peers, and supervisors.

In each negotiation, information, time, and power are the crucial variables to be considered. In the process of negotiation, attention must be focused on the problems and the interests of each party. It is important that each party assertively state his or her own interests. By creating multiple options and then examining them with objective criteria, the most workable solutions can be created. Win–win negotiation is based on the understanding that both parties share fundamentally compatible goals and neither desires to harm the other.

☐ Conclusion

By being assertive and negotiating solutions with all levels of health care personnel, nurse managers play active roles in redesigning the health care system. It has become an everyday occurrence for nurse managers to negotiate for the resources needed to provide quality patient care and to negotiate with staff for new role definitions. As more nonprofessionals join the health care team, it is crucial for nurse managers to delegate and teach delegation skills to staff. Sharing responsibility and authority and supporting staff in their accountability for patient care outcomes fosters a patient-centered, quality care approach. By being a role model and teaching delegation, nurse managers empower their staffs. The four skills described in this chapter—delegation, conflict resolution, assertiveness, and negotiation—enable nurse managers to effectively lead their staff in the ever-changing health care arena.

☐ References

1. Rowland, H., and Rowland, B. *Nursing Administration Handbook.* Germantown, MD: Aspen Systems Corporation, 1980.

2. Baldwin, B. The dynamics of delegation: sharing responsibility effectively. *Piedmont Airlines,* pp. 6, 13–18, 22, 1985.

3. Hart, L. *Learning from Conflict.* Reading, MA: Addison-Wesley Publishing Co., 1981.

4. Cohen, H. *You Can Negotiate Anything.* Secaucus, NJ: Kyle Stuart, 1980.

5. Karrass, C. L. *The Negotiating Game.* New York City: Thomas Y. Crowell Co., 1970.

6. Cohen, 1980.

7. Cohen, 1980.

8. Karrass, 1970.

9. Fisher, R., and Ury, W. *Getting to Yes: Negotiating Agreement without Giving In.* New York City: Penguin Books, 1983.

☐ *Bibliography*

Alberti, R., and Emmons, M. *Your Perfect Right.* San Luis Obispo, CA: Impact Press, 1970.

Angle, G., and Knox-Petronko, D. *Developing the New Assertive Nurse.* New York City: Springer Publishing Co., 1983.

Baer, J. *How to Be an Assertive (Not Aggressive) Woman in Life, in Love, and on the Job.* New York City: Signet, 1976.

Bolton, R. *People Skills.* Englewood Cliffs, NJ: Prentice-Hall, 1979.

Cialdine, R. *Influence: How and Why People Agree to Things.* New York City: Morrow, 1984.

Cohen, A., and Bradford, D. *Influence without Authority.* New York City: John Wiley, 1990.

Fensterheim, H., and Baer, J. *Don't Say Yes When You Want to Say No.* New York City: Dell Publishing Co., 1975.

Filley, A. C. *Interpersonal Conflict Resolution.* Glenview, IL: Scott, Foresman & Co., 1975.

Grossman, R. Talking straight: how to say no without hurting anyone. *Health* 15(2):8–26, 1983.

Jernigan, D., and Young, A. *Standards, Job Descriptions, and Performance Evaluations for Nursing Practice.* Norwalk, CT: Appleton-Century-Crofts, 1983.

Kelley, J. A. Negotiating skills for the nursing service administrator. *Nursing Clinics of North America* 18(3):427–38, Sept. 1983.

McFarland, G. K., Skipton-Leonard, M., and Morris, N. M. Conflict and conflict management. In: *Nursing Leadership and Management: Contemporary Strategy.* New York City: John Wiley & Sons, 1984.

Manthey, M. The role of the LPN or . . . the problem of two levels. *Nursing Management* 20(2):26, 28, Feb. 1989.

Murphy, E. C. Delegation—from denial to acceptance. *Nursing Management* 15:54–56, 1984.

Peters, T. *Thriving on Chaos: A Handbook on Management Revolution.* New York City: Random House, 1987.

Peterson, M. E. Motivating staff to participate in decision making. *Nursing Administration Quarterly* 7(2):63–68, Winter 1983.

Poteet, G. W. Delegation strategies: a must for the nurse executive. *Journal of Nursing Administration* 14:18–21, 1984.

Poteet, G. W. Delegation strategies for the pediatric nurse. *Journal of Pediatric Nursing* 1:271–73, 1986.

Raiffa, H. *The Art and Science of Negotiation.* Cambridge, MA: Beknap Press, 1982.

Simpson, K., and Sears, R. Authority and responsibility delegation predicts quality of care. *Journal of Advanced Nursing* 10:345–48, 1985.

Smith, M. *When I Say No I Feel Guilty.* New York City: Dial Press, 1975.

Sovie, M. Redesigning our future: whose responsibility is it? *Nursing Economics* 8(1):21–26, 1990.

Taubman, B. *How to Become an Assertive Woman.* New York City: Pocket Books, 1976.

Zemke, R. Conflict resolution: fighting off the urge to fight on. *Training* 7:38–40, 1981.

Chapter 3

Creating and Maintaining a High-Performance Team

*Julie W. Schaffner, R.N., M.S.N.,
and Martha Bermingham, R.N., M.M.*

A nurse manager is only as successful as his or her team. Creating and maintaining a high-performance team is a key to management and organizational success. A high-performance team functions synergistically and views teamwork as a high priority. Team members are highly motivated and strive for continuous improvement. They also support each other, openly address conflicts and issues, and mentor and coach new staff.

Creating a high-performance team can lower staff vacancy and turnover rates as well as increase staff morale and patient satisfaction. A team that feels good about itself and its ability to work together has a positive impact on the delivery of patient care. In addition, building a high-performance team provides the nurse manager with intrinsic and extrinsic rewards—personal satisfaction along with recognition from administration, physicians, patients, and families.

This chapter presents techniques for building a high-performance team by creating a culture of high performance through the selection and retention of talented staff and improvement of work processes.

Creating a high-performance team is unlikely without a strong culture that supports innovation and change and rewards outstanding performance. The next section provides a basis for understanding hospitalwide, nursing-service, and unit-level culture and describes approaches for assessing and transforming culture at the nursing service and unit level.

☐ Understanding Corporate Culture

Understanding corporate culture is critical to determining why a nursing unit or nursing service is dysfunctional. Nurse managers and nurse executives must understand how corporate culture shapes an organization, how to identify the appropriate corporate culture, and how to communicate that culture to the staff.

How Is Corporate Culture Defined?

Corporate culture can be defined as the personality of the hospital, nursing service, or unit. This *personality*—its common beliefs, values, and assumptions—shapes institutional behavior and sets norms. Every day the culture is passed along to each employee as "the way we do things around here." Most often, these processes have worked in the past, and they maintain consistent behavior and decision making among staff. Corporate culture bonds a nursing unit or nursing service together. Accepting corporate culture provides meaning, direction, and purpose for staff at all levels.

Corporate culture starts at the top of the organization and cascades downward. Separate and distinct cultures often exist within nursing service. Subcultures exist at the unit level. Although it would be ideal, it is rare that one strong corporate culture exists throughout the organization as a whole.

Understanding the organization's culture is the first step in attempting to understand the unit culture. A great deal can be learned by reviewing the written vision, mission, values, and philosophy for both the organization and nursing service. The manager also learns by observing the behavior of top administration and other managers and noting their consistency with the organization's values. Discussing corporate culture with management and staff can also be enlightening for the manager.

Is There a Correct Unit Culture?

There is no *right* or *wrong* nursing unit culture. What is important is for the nurse manager to create a unit culture that fits comfortably and appropriately with the culture of nursing services and the organization. For example, if the nursing service has evolved into a decentralized structure valuing participative management and consensus while the unit subculture values directive management, the two cultures will clash. It is important that the cultures fit synergistically. If there is a conflict between these internal cultures, performance will suffer. For the manager's personal satisfaction and the development of a high-performance team, there must be a cultural synergy among the unit, nursing service, and the organization.

How Is Culture Communicated within the Organization?

Corporate culture is communicated in many ways at all levels of the organization. Senior management communicates corporate culture through written mission, vision, value, and philosophy statements. Organizational activities, policies, procedures, and management behavior also communicate corporate culture.

The nursing service often has a distinct culture, which may differ from that of the corporate. Again, the culture is communicated through written materials, such as vision, mission, and nursing philosophy statements. Day-to-day behavior, leadership meeting agendas, and department priorities also will indicate nursing service culture. For example, at a department meeting it is easy for an individual to ascertain whether clinical managers are empowered to make decisions or whether the power is held by senior nursing leadership. Managers also will be able to determine if creativity, innovation, and risk taking are valued. By observing, listening, and asking questions, managers will begin to understand the department's personality and "how things are done."

Nursing management should ensure that the mission, vision, and values of the organization are ingrained in the nursing service culture through written communications. In addition, all the organization's activities should support the mission and vision. Although values (for example, respect, collaboration, creativity, and stewardship) can also be distributed in writing, they are more effectively communicated through the behavior of role models.

Culture at the unit level may be strong, weak, or fragmented and may or may not support the culture of the organization and/or nursing service. Unit culture is communicated through the following mechanisms:

- *Rites, rituals, and ceremonies.* For example, completing nursing orientation is a rite of passage. What orientees have to do to become accepted members of the team communicates a great deal about the unit culture. Are they still considered new staff nurses, even after they have worked for a year? Are they tested repeatedly on their clinical knowledge or accepted at face value due to past experience? Rituals at the unit level may include attending shift report meeting, wearing caps, making beds on the day shift, and taking breaks with the same people at the same time every day.
- *Role models.* The unit culture will determine who becomes a role model. Is it the clinical expert, the informal leader, or the clinical manager? What makes a staff member a hero or heroine? Is it the dramatic resuscitation of a newborn baby or the way a nurse stood up to administration?
- *Stories.* Stories bond staff members together into a team. They communicate unit values, beliefs, and traditions. Stories may relate to unusual patients, difficult physicians, and blizzards that kept the staff stranded for days.

- *Rewards.* Culture is communicated by how and for what staff are recognized and rewarded at the unit level. For example, who is selected for a promotion, who is permitted to attend a symposium, or who is asked to serve on an important committee?

Before formally assessing the unit culture, the manager should informally observe behavior and staff interactions. The manager should ask him or herself whether the values, mission, and vision of the organization or nursing service are understood and/or demonstrated at the unit level. What is the unit's focus? Also, the relationship between managers and staff must be evaluated. If the types of new strategies intended for implementation do not seem compatible with what is observed at the unit level, the likelihood of success is minimal unless the culture is transformed.

☐ Conducting a Formal Cultural Assessment

After gaining a basic understanding of the culture at various levels of the organization, the nurse manager is ready to initiate a more formal assessment. If the hospital administration is committed to change and the culture of the nursing service or the unit is not compatible with the institution's strategic direction, a formal cultural assessment is a crucial first step toward change. The means of approaching assessment are the same for both the nursing service and the unit:

1. Choose the components (characteristics, behaviors, and activities) that illustrate the current culture.
2. Develop and distribute a questionnaire based on these components.
3. Analyze the results of the questionnaire and communicate them to the staff.

What Are the Steps in Nursing Service Cultural Assessment?

A nursing service cultural assessment will give the nurse manager valuable information on the common beliefs and practices within and throughout the nursing department. The following subsections describe the steps as they apply to the nursing service.

Choose the Components

Many components of corporate culture may be evaluated during a nursing service cultural assessment. Each component is a characteristic, behavior, or activity that illustrates the culture in the institution. Examples of components of culture particularly helpful in developing assessment tools include:

- Involvement and participation
- Decision making
- Motivation of staff
- Presence of rites, rituals, and ceremonies
- Value of creativity and innovation
- Power and authority
- Conflict and conflict resolution
- Allocation of resources (human and fiscal) to nursing
- Ability to change
- Communication methods
- Degree of teamwork

Every institution should develop its own list of components. When choosing the components, a nurse manager should ask himself or herself what information would encourage insight into the culture and what would be important to the nursing service? A manager may generate a list of components by compiling a literature review or brainstorming with key nurse executives or members of the nursing staff.

Develop and Implement a Questionnaire

A team of senior and middle-level nurse managers should use the components, and any other relevant information, to develop a questionnaire. In order to focus the process, no more than 20 characteristics should be selected. The team should choose three questions for each component. The questions should address the present culture in terms of how it is viewed by the staff, what is desired for the future, and which strategies will move the organization in the desired direction.

For example, if the component were power and authority, the three questions might be these:

1. Who has the power and authority in the nursing service?
2. Who should have the power and authority in the nursing service?
3. What strategies will move power and authority to the person it belongs with, as identified in question 2?

Questions should be put into workbook format. It is also important that the workbook be prefaced with a verbal or written summation of the vision, mission, and values of the hospital and nursing services, along with the purpose of the assessment and what it is intended to accomplish. The workbook should be distributed to a cross section of staff members –

that is, nurses from all specialties, shifts, and levels of experience. The cross section should also represent various degrees of tenure, age, ethnic background, and education. Workbooks must be kept confidential and anonymous.

If feasible, a nurse manager should take selected staff on a several-day-long retreat during which workbooks could be completed rapidly. If this is not practical, the manager should identify a time frame or due date that the workbooks should be returned. Figure 3-1 is an excerpt from a hospital's cultural assessment workbook. The excerpt includes the hospital's philosophy and mission statements, a list of the components of the culture to be assessed, and sample questions.

Analyze the Results

In order to maintain consistency in the way the results are written up, a single individual should analyze the workbooks. This person may be a manager, a staff analyst, or a staff development instructor. Workbooks should be reviewed for common themes as well as for gaps between the present and the desired culture. The resulting information can then be tabulated.

For example, the staff may repeatedly identify its lack of involvement in decision making. If staff members wanted more involvement in decision making, implementing shared governance within the nursing service might be recommended. Figure 3-2 (p. 64) illustrates this and other sample themes that might be found during the data analysis stage.

The last and most crucial step in performing a cultural assessment is to distribute the results of the questionnaire to the staff. In open forums, staff should discuss the validity of the information presented and make recommendations for action. This feedback serves as the basis for the transformation plan.

What Are the Steps in Unit-Level Cultural Assessment?

A unit-level cultural assessment is necessary when major change is to be introduced, particularly if an informal assessment by the manager and staff clearly demonstrates that the unit culture is weak and fragmented or that it does not fit into the culture of the nursing service or the organization. It is also critical to ascertain whether the nursing service culture is supported by and viewed as a positive force in the organization. It would be difficult to successfully perform a unit-based cultural assessment within a nursing service culture that was dysfunctional overall. Before beginning a unit-based cultural assessment, it is important that the nurse manager obtain sponsorship from his or her superior. Due to the time, energy, and resources needed for cultural transformation,

Figure 3-1. Excerpt from a Hospital's Cultural Assessment Workbook

A. Nursing: Vision Statement

We are committed to the philosophy of human ecology. We care for the whole person: mind, body, and spirit. The patient and the family are the center of our professional practice. We promote the well-being of our patients and their families through compassionate quality care.

We are accountable for professional nursing practice which provides a patient advocacy role that impacts patient satisfaction, continuity of care, physician/nurse collaboration and appropriate resource allocation. We believe our role extends beyond the geographical boundaries of the hospital, and recognize our responsibility to participate in meeting the health and educational needs of the community we serve.

As a nationally recognized center for nursing excellence, we are committed to a professional practice environment in which autonomy, collaboration, and mutual respect are essential. Creativity and innovation are supported and rewarded. We recognize the valuable contributions nurses make to health care.

We contribute to the knowledge base of nursing practice and health care through promoting education, research and collaboration. We provide care based on standards of practice that promote ethical decision making.

B. Nursing: Mission Statement

We will provide coordinated patient and family centered care that is recognized as the best in the Chicago area. We will continue to support a system that values innovative nursing care delivery and enhances the quality of care in a cost effective manner.

We will identify ethical dilemmas and address them in a responsible manner.

We will promote collaborative relationships with physicians and other colleagues in order to assure high quality patient care delivery.

We will implement strategies that support professional practice while encouraging innovative ideas and decision making.

We will manage change effectively, in order to maximize opportunities and minimize dangers.

We will provide a climate conducive to learning which stimulates inquiry and creative problem solving.

We are committed to make Lutheran General Hospital the employer of choice for nursing and a model for other hospitals.

We will work together as a team and take pride in our accomplishments.

We will utilize our resources in a responsible manner to best serve the health care needs of our community, now and in the future.

C. Components of Culture To Be Assessed

1. Purpose
2. Organizational Structure
3. Results Orientation
4. Technology
5. Change Orientation
6. Change Implementation
7. Leadership
8. Power
9. Decision Making
10. Urgency
11. Commitment
12. Nursing Involvement
13. Crisis Management
14. Attention

(continued on next page)

Figure 3-1. (Continued)

15. Performance Appraisal	26. Employment Policies
16. Motivation	27. Orientation and Training
17. Compensation	28. Creativity
18. Resource Utilization	29. Success
19. Accountability	30. Work Habits
20. Communication	31. Pride
21. Openness	32. Ethics
22. Conflict	33. Initiative
23. Teamwork	34. Ceremonies
24. Individual Image	35. Rights and Rituals
25. Facilities	36. Symbols

D. Sample of Questions

16. Motivation:
   A: How are nurses motivated in the existing nursing culture? For example, are incentives used or pressures applied?

   _____

   _____

   _____

   _____

   B: To succeed in the future, what should the culture imply about how incentives and pressures may be used?

   _____

   _____

   _____

   C: How should staff be motivated in the future?

   _____

   _____

   _____

   _____

20. Communication:
   A: How does the existing nursing culture influence communication? That is, what is communicated, to whom and when does it occur?

   _____

   _____

   _____

   _____

Figure 3-1. (Continued)

B: To succeed in the future, how should the nursing culture influence communication?

_____

_____

_____

_____

C: What strategies should be utilized to improve communication in nursing?

_____

_____

_____

_____

23. Teamwork:
    A: How is teamwork encouraged by the present nursing culture (for example, within units, shift-to-shift, between units or sections)?

_____

_____

_____

_____

B: To succeed in the future, how should the nursing culture emphasize teamwork within nursing?

_____

_____

_____

_____

C: What should be done to improve or enhance teamwork within nursing?

_____

_____

_____

_____

Reprinted, with permission, from Lutheran General Hospital, Park Ridge, Illinois.

Figure 3-2. Sample Results of a Data Analysis

Present State	Desired State	Recommendations
Power vested in vice-president and nursing directors	Staff empowerment	Implement shared governance
Lack of recognition of nursing	Recognition of nursing contribution	Celebrate contribution of nursing through newsletters, awards, and ceremonies
Creativity not fostered	Environment that fosters creativity	Reward and recognize creativity and utilize pilot approach to try creative ideas
Hospital too focused on the bottom line	Patient-centered focus	Adopt patient-centered care hospitalwide

sponsorship from the organization's senior levels is a crucial factor in any success. In addition, without *visible* support from senior management, resistance and sabotage are more likely to occur.

Choose the Components

First, the components of the culture that are relevant at the unit level are selected. The clans or subgroups working on the unit are then identified. Subgroups come from a cross section of staff by shift, tenure, education, position, ethnic background, and age. Randomly selecting staff or requesting volunteers may be problematic if specific subgroups are left out. Without acknowledging the various subgroups and the components that affect them, the cultural assessment will be incomplete and data skewed.

Each subculture tends to operate under its own rules. In addition, these subcultures have their own values. If there is a conflict, members are more likely to follow subculture rather than organizational values. Subcultures are powerful groups, and attempting to change their values can lead to a revolt. For example, a subculture value within an all registered nurse day shift might be "personalized, hands-on care." When financial constraints force a skill-mix change, values are threatened and high turnover is likely to result. The component list should reflect these values.

Possible unit-level components include:

- Power
- Decision making
- Nursing staff involvement
- Resource utilization
- Work habits
- Orientation and training

- Communication
- Conflict management
- Teamwork
- Ethics

Develop and Implement a Questionnaire

After choosing the components, the manager's next step is to develop a questionnaire. In order to give the process a strong focus, no more than 10 components should be selected. A focus group of staff members may be utilized to identify the components to be assessed. As for the nursing service cultural assessment, three questions should be developed for each of the 10 components. For example:

1. How is conflict currently handled on the unit?
2. How should conflict be handled?
3. What strategies will move conflict management to where it should be, as suggested in question 2?

The manager should select representatives from all the subcultures to complete the questionnaire. All staff members can be classified into at least one group according to tenure, shift, age, ethnic background, education, position, and so forth.

Analyze the Results

The nurse manager should analyze the results, identify themes, and prepare tables (similar to that shown in figure 3-2) describing the unit's present and desired state, as well as recommendations for change. Staff should discuss and validate the results in open forums. Forums build consensus and allow staff to choose a theme on which they wish to focus. At these meetings, staff should select volunteers to work on each theme. They should decide on time frames, develop reporting methodology, and ensure that there are communication mechanisms between management and the staff.

☐ Transforming the Culture

After the data are collected and analyzed, there are several options on how to proceed. The nurse manager may decide to ignore the culture, manage around it, or attempt to alter management strategies to fit into the culture. Although these options may work in the short term, they will not enable the nurse manager to create a culture that motivates a high-performance team. Without a high-performance team, the manager will not be able to manage successfully over the long term. Change will not be sustained—burnout will result and personal satisfaction will be minimal. The only approach that ensures long-term success and the ability to create and sustain a high-performance team is to accept the challenge of cultural transformation.

Cultural transformation is neither easy nor magical. It requires time, patience, creativity, strong interpersonal and negotiation skills, and senior-level support and sponsorship. Transforming the culture of a unit is easier than transforming that of the nursing service because it is smaller in size and scope. No matter which area is transformed, however, managers must serve as role models and catalysts for change.

The same type of approach to change may be used for the nursing service and the unit. The nurse manager must keep in mind, however, that both communication and action are more difficult to implement when dealing with the nursing service. Sheer numbers, coupled with numerous shifts and personal agendas, contribute to the difficulty of the task. Strategic planning is an approach that will be helpful in cultural transformation. Often, the results of a cultural assessment may serve to underpin the planning or adapting of new processes within nursing. Ideally, gaps between the present and desired state provide opportunities to identify strategies for change within the nursing service. Initiating and implementing specific tactics that delineate these strategies, along with methods for evaluating success, complete the process. Again, senior nursing leadership must be committed to transformation, and the support of hospital administration is mandatory.

To use a cultural assessment for strategic planning, a nurse manager can review the assessment results and then identify, from the staff's perspective, any gaps between desire and reality. Without understanding these gaps, transformation will not be possible. The manager can ignore the components that show the present and desired states to be the same. By concentrating on those components that reflect gaps between reality and desire, the nurse manager will be able to effect the greatest impact.

Staff must be involved in developing the strategies that will move the nursing service or unit from the present to the desired state. First, general goals and objectives and second, specific work steps, accountabilities, time frames, and monitoring mechanisms must be identified. Managers must set stretch goals for their teams. As mentioned earlier, the manager and the team should concentrate on the areas with the greatest gap between the present state and the desired state. It is important that time frames for transformation be realistic. True cultural transformation takes years, but dramatic improvement in team performance can be seen along the way. Below are two examples that demonstrate the transformation process in action:

- *Example 1.* In a nursing service, the present state may reflect a lack of communication between staff and management. The desired state is to receive more communication. The assessment recommendation suggests more effective communication strategies, such as monthly staff meetings, a monthly newsletter from nursing administration, and written minutes of meetings to be distributed to each unit for posting. More specific tactics (see figure 3-3) delineate who is responsible for each strategy, the time frame for implementation, the work steps necessary to accomplish the strategies, and a method by which strategies and tactics are evaluated.
- *Example 2.* The present state may also reflect a lack of communication at the unit level. The desired state is one characterized by improved communication. Recommendations include monthly staff meetings with minutes, a new format for shift report, and a bulletin board dedicated to posting nursing announcements and information. Again, more specific tactics delineating accountabilities, work steps, and evaluation methods should be identified.

When selecting the specific themes on which to concentrate the transformation, a nurse manager needs to be realistic about what can be accomplished. When three to five action plans have been selected and implemented, the transformation process has begun.

The role of managers in cultural transformation is to coach, mentor, and counsel. They monitor the progress and provide rewards and recognition as the effort progresses. Staff will need to be constantly reminded of how much time it takes for true cultural transformation to occur. Resources external to the unit should be provided for the staff as needed. These may include assistance from the human resource and/or the education and training departments.

Figure 3-3. Strategy: Improve Communication within Nursing

Tactics	Accountability	Time Frame	Evaluation
1. Establish monthly staff meetings	Manager	Within one month	Feedback from staff on meeting contents via survey
2. Distribute monthly newsletter from nursing administration	Director	Within three months	Newsletter on all units
3. Distribute minutes of meetings	Shared governance representative	Within two months	Minutes posted on bulletin board within five days of meeting

In addition, the strength of the subcultures must be evaluated and incorporated into the transformation process. For example, if specific subcultures are having a negative impact on the unit, an action plan must be developed to address the issue. The nurse manager needs to determine what is important to each subculture. This can be done by asking people what they consider to be the important aspects of their work or what quality means to them. Utilizing this information, the nurse manager makes the subgroups part of the transformation process by involving them in strategies. For example, if subcultures, such as day staff and evening staff, are engaging in open warfare, the manager can put them together on a project with a common goal. If subculture values are in conflict with organizational values, the manager can identify strategies to integrate the two. Often, cultural transformation and positive change at the unit level will change the behavior and norms of the various subcultures.

Along the road to cultural transformation, communicating frequently with staff on the status of strategies is the nurse manager's most important tool for success. The nurse manager should also celebrate successes with the staff and discuss obstacles and revise strategies, if indicated. The staff should understand that strategies are not set in stone but serve as adjustable guidelines for change.

☐ Choosing the Right People

If the first component of creating a high-performance team is securing a culture of high performance, the second component is choosing and retaining the right people. Recruiting, motivating, and retaining appropriate staff is critical to high performance. A unit comprised of people who do not fit in or ascribe to the culture will not function synergistically. This section explores how to recruit the right staff, and the subsequent section discusses how to motivate and retain current staff.

How Can a Manager Recruit the Right Staff?

Recruiting the right staff is one of the most challenging and important tasks a manager faces. There may be applicants who are technically qualified but for other reasons are not appropriate for a position. For example, someone whose values differ from those of the institution will not be a good candidate. The process of recruiting staff who are technically qualified *and* who will enhance the unit's performance involves three steps:

- Creating a job description
- Using effective recruitment techniques
- Interviewing effectively

Create a Job Description

The search for a candidate must start with a well-conceived job description. This description must spell out the position's duties and responsibilities as well as the qualifications and values sought in a successful candidate. As described earlier, the culture of the unit is critical to its performance. Therefore, the values held by the candidate will determine whether that individual will be an asset or a liability to the culture of the unit. A job description (as fully illustrated in figure 3-4) should include the following components:

- Position title
- Reporting and supervisory relationships
- General summary
- Duties and responsibilities, including stated values of the organization
- Educational requirements

A clear, specific job description articulating tasks and expectations is useful for both the employer and potential employee. Employers must be clear in what they need and expect of employees; employees must be able to see what is expected of them. When duties and responsibilities are clear, the skills required for the position can be determined more easily.

The job description should also incorporate, in very concrete terms, the organization's values, thereby notifying the potential employee that these values are real and part of the job, not just words on paper. When the organization's values are incorporated into the job description, not only are the duties and skills identified, but also the characteristics of the successful health care practitioner.

Use Effective Recruitment Techniques

In order to select the right person, the nurse manager must recruit enough candidates to have a reasonable choice. Ineffective recruitment will yield an inadequate supply of candidates from which to choose. Effective recruitment will increase the probability of finding the right person.

Recruitment is the art of notifying potential candidates of the opportunity being offered. There are various ways to alert potential candidates—advertising, job fairs, direct mailing, networking, and so forth.

Although it can be expensive and complicated, *advertising* is the most common method of communicating with the public. Various hospital departments are invaluable in identifying the best places to

Figure 3-4.   Position Description: Registered Nurse

I. Position Identification
Position Title: Registered Nurse

II. Position Relationships
Reports to: Director of Nursing

III. General Summary

Provides nursing care to assigned patients by demonstrating general nursing knowledge through application of the nursing process specific to assessment, planning, implementation, and evaluation of the plan. Implements the philosophy of human ecology. Leadership abilities are demonstrated in functioning as a professional role model.

IV. Duties and Responsibilities

A. Professional Development/Organization Standards Demonstrates behaviors promoting professional growth.

1. Incorporates the following values:
   - Respect—Regard for self, colleagues, and others.
   - Servanthood—An understanding of service that calls for a personal and communal commitment to unselfishly care for others.
   - Creativity—Innovative thinking, planning, and implementation. Compatible with our vision requiring flexibility, responsiveness, and willingness to change.
   - Collaboration—Effective cooperation that recognizes that each person, service or business is part of the whole and is integral and essential to the fulfillment of the mission.

2. Accepts professional responsibility and participates in activities that further develop professional growth.

3. Incorporates information and skills acquired in learning activities to improve patient care.

4. Completes assignments within the scheduled hours of work.

5. Complies with policies and procedures established by the hospital and specific division.

B. Assessment of Patients

Demonstrates the ability to appropriately assess the patient in a systematic way to promote optimal level of wellness. Documents patient assessment and teaching needs.

1. Assesses patient in systematic way and documents appropriately.

2. Interviews and obtains patient history utilizing direct and indirect sources of data.

3. Formulates nursing diagnoses through the identification of the patient's nursing problems.

4. Identifies learning needs of patients and families.

5. Identifies potential/actual discharge needs.

6. Initiates referrals to the health care team.

7. Identifies changes in patient's condition and takes appropriate actions.

C. Plan

Plans nursing care based on sound nursing principles. Documents plans according to policy and procedure.

Figure 3-4. (Continued)

1. Develops individualized nursing care plans and establishes priorities for patient care based on medical and nursing diagnoses.

2. Identifies realistic goals related to patient's physiological and psychosocial needs.

3. Develops and/or implements appropriate teaching plans in accordance with the plan of care.

4. Involves patient and/or family in the plan of care.

5. Incorporates suggestions of staff associated in planning care.

6. Identifies need for and participates in patient care conferences/multidisciplinary team conferences.

7. Throughout hospitalization, incorporates discharge planning in the nursing plan of care.

8. Initiates interaction with other members of the health care team for the purpose of coordinating direct patient care efforts and/or operating as the patient's advocate.

D. Implementation

Provides nursing care for optimal levels of wellness for each patient and documents such care according to policy and procedure.

1. Engages in safe nursing practice for patient, family, and members of the health care team.

2. Prioritizes the patient's daily needs in order to plan for optimum level of care.

3. Seeks input from patient and family in planning patient care.

4. Actively participates in patient and multidisciplinary team conferences.

5. Utilizes available resources both within and outside the institution for the purpose of providing optimum comprehensive nursing care for both patient and family.

6. Implements, utilizes, and revises the nursing care plan to reflect current and changing status of the patient.

E. Evaluation

Demonstrates abilities to evaluate and revise plan of care as needed. Documents such according to policy and procedure.

1. Evaluates effectiveness of nursing interventions.

2. Reassesses the patient's short- and long-term goals related to the patient and family's physiological and psychosocial needs.

3. Consistently modifies care plan to meet patient needs and goals.

4. Evaluates effectiveness of patient care/therapies incorporating suggestions/ideas of staff associates.

5. Consistently validates nursing decisions and actions demonstrating flexibility, innovation, and increasing proficiency.

6. Assesses the patient's progress toward health goals and offers additional or alternative plans of care.

V. Educational Requirements

Licensed as a registered professional nurse in the state of Illinois. Successful completion of basic nursing education.

Reprinted, with permission, from Lutheran General Hospital, Park Ridge, Illinois.

advertise. For example, marketing and human resources know the local health care recruitment publications and newspapers that will yield the best results. Although these departments can help in the placement of the ads, the nurse manager must describe the content of what is to be communicated.

Unless an advertisement clearly describes a position, as well as the qualifications required, money is wasted. In working with the department placing the ads, the nurse manager helps create and review ads. An advertisement attracts a candidate's attention by clearly stating the qualifications being sought and identifying the advantages of the institution over others. Important components of successful advertisements include:

- An accurate job title
- The requirements of the successful candidate (for example, baccalaureate degree or specific IV therapy experience)
- The personal and professional characteristics sought (for example, patient advocate or self-starter)
- The benefits of the institution (for example, tuition reimbursement or teaching hospital environment)

The following items should *not* be included in an advertisement:

- Specific pay
- Promises that the manager may not be able to keep (for example, special shifts or preferential scheduling)
- Such general requirements that anyone is eligible (for example, graduate nurse)
- Discriminatory requirements (for example, male nurses needed)
- Too many positions so that it appears as though there is a problem with getting and keeping staff

Advertising in local health care recruitment publications and newspapers is one way to communicate to potential employees. Although this method of communication works well, there are other paths to successful recruitment.

Job fairs are also a good way to recruit staff as they expose large numbers of potential candidates to personal representatives of an institution. Both new graduates and experienced staff frequent job fairs and can learn a great deal about what an institution has to offer. It is best to have human resource and nursing representatives at a job fair. Each has different areas of expertise providing potential candidates with an overall view of what to expect. Going to job fairs helps managers become more aware of what other institutions are offering and how competitive their institution is in the community.

Direct mailings to nurses within the community are another way to recruit. Typically, these mailings are about opportunities in general and would not be used to advertise specific positions. Direct mailings are usually managed by the marketing department, but the nursing service should review the content.

Networking, or the informal communication of employment opportunities, is a very effective way to recruit. Referrals can be encouraged with an internal bonus system. There are a number of ways to communicate employment opportunities to staff:

- Job bulletin boards
- Announcements at staff meetings
- Newsletters about nursing issues, including job opportunities
- Peer interaction

Often, more jobs are filled through a "referral from a friend" than through any other single method of communication.

Finally, reviewing past candidate and recruitment records can provide valuable information. How did candidates learn of opportunities? Each recruiting effort should have a follow-up report that describes its effectiveness. How many candidates were generated? How many were successful candidates? How much did it cost? What was the cost per hire? Reports on the success of various recruiting techniques will be very useful in providing data to support more effective recruitment strategies in the future.

Interview Effectively

Interviewing is a time-consuming and, therefore, expensive process. It requires the manager's, candidates', and human resource personnel's time. For these reasons, it is important that the process of selecting candidates be designed in such a way that there are mechanisms to screen out unqualified candidates. Ideally, human resource personnel should read and screen all candidate resumés, thereby ensuring that the candidates interviewed have met the criteria set jointly by the manager and human resource personnel. Of the resumés that come to the institution, only a small percentage should result in personal interviews with the manager.

Interviewing for the "right" candidate involves two steps:

- Identifying the specific behaviors for successful job performance
- Asking the questions to ascertain whether the candidate will behave in the desired way

Identifying the specific behaviors is the first step. In recruiting a staff nurse, for example, the manager refers to a job description that articulates the duties, responsibilities, and values involved in the position. In addition, the manager feels the successful candidate must demonstrate certain behaviors. One of these behaviors is flexibility. Therefore, the nurse manager will need to create questions that will elicit answers from the candidate that help the manager determine whether the candidate is flexible.

For example, the manager might inquire about the candidate's former schedule: "How did you manage your schedule in your last job? How were scheduling conflicts resolved? Can you give examples of times that the schedule was difficult to resolve? How did you do it?" The answers to these questions would give the manager valuable insight into how the candidate might behave in the future. If the candidate were to say that scheduling conflicts were resolved by applying a policy statement, that would give the manager a sense of the candidate's possible inflexibility. If the candidate said that the conflicts were resolved by compromise, the manager might get a different sense of the candidate's ability to be flexible.

Following are some practical guidelines for interviewing that help interviewers learn more about the candidate and help the candidate learn more about the open position, the manager, and the institution:

1. Speak with candidates yourself before the interview to arrange the time and place. This will give candidates a sense that you are interested in them.
2. Give candidates your undivided attention. Allow about 30 minutes of uninterrupted interview time in a quiet place where you will not be disturbed. Follow the interview with a short tour of the unit if the candidate seems promising.
3. Make candidates feel at ease by beginning with small talk to relax them; for example, "Thank you for coming. Did you have any trouble finding the hospital?"
4. Make candidates feel at ease by identifying with them; for example, "I see from your resumé that you graduated from the University of Illinois. So did I."
5. Maximize your time together. Become familiar with the candidate's background before the interview, and plan the questions that you will ask.
6. Clarify any discrepancies on the resumé, such as inconsistencies in dates or years unaccounted for. Also clarify the responsibilities for each position listed on the resumé.
7. Assess why the candidate left his or her previous position. Listen for a sense of discontentment. Does he or she malign a former employer? Does he or she give positive reasons for changing jobs? Red flags might include: "My last place was disorganized," or "We had a personality

conflict," or "I felt stifled." A positive attitude in the workplace is important to a high-performance unit. A person who is negative about a former employment situation may potentially be negative about other employment situations.

8. Ask what the candidate is looking for. You need to know concrete information, such as pay and hours, but also subjective requirements, such as experience and desire for growth.

9. Provide the following information about the position and the institution. The following lead-ins may prove helpful:
   - "Let me tell you about the position." (Always provide the candidate a copy of the job description.)
   - "Let me tell you about the organization." (Discuss strategic goals, values, strengths, and growth areas.)
   - "Let me show you the unit." (Introduce the candidate to selected staff members.)
   - "Let me tell you what I am looking for." (List the personal characteristics that will make a person successful in the position.)

10. Learn as much as you can about the individual personally. Ask the candidate to tell you about himself or herself. What candidates choose to tell you will say a lot about them.

Some managers might like to interview a candidate with several other staff members present. Other managers, after the initial interview, may have the candidate interview with selected staff. These types of interviews can be beneficial to the selection process. In a highly developed shared governance environment, peer interviews are a good way for candidates and units to verify the fit.

Evaluate the Recruitment Efforts

There are two ways to assess a recruitment activity's success rate— measuring how long it takes to fill a position and/or how successful the candidate is after a predefined period of employment.

The time it takes to fill a position is a very subjective measurement. For example, when the manager is recruiting for one empty night nurse position, a week may be a long time. However, if a position has been open for a long time relative to others in the hospital, one week may not be very long.

After a predetermined period of employment are there problems? For example, is an employee taking the usual amount of time to orient? Is this individual proving to be a team player? Did this individual stay with the institution a reasonable length of time? If no, the recruitment records should be reviewed for missed red flags. This will help the manager to avoid problems with future recruitments.

☐ Motivating the Staff to High Performance

Recruiting the right staff is the first step in managing human resources. The next step is motivating that staff to high performance. Motivating staff to high performance will depend to a large extent on the manager's ability to instill the hospital's vision, mission, values, and direction into the work performed every day. A staff is motivated to excellence when it has a clear sense of common goals and an understanding of how the staff contributes to the success of the hospital.

There are three strategies for motivating staff: (1) providing direction through strategic planning, (2) applying participative management strategies, and (3) rewarding behavior.

What Role Does Strategic Planning Play?

Most hospitals have a mission, vision, and values statement that serves as the basis of planning processes. The strategic planning process translates the mission, vision, and values into action. Strategic planning starts at the top and flows throughout the organization. Without a common set of strategies, staff may become unfocused and unsure of the organization's priorities. Staff members need to understand how they fit into and affect the organization's overall plan.

In many hospitals, the executive staff and the board of trustees develop a strategic plan to help guide the organization and establish a clear sense of direction. The vice-president of nursing or patient care services is usually involved at this level. Some nursing services establish their own strategic plan that flows from the hospital's plan. Both strategic plans should be utilized, if available, as nurse managers prepare goals and objectives for the unit and staff.

The strategic planning process flows through the organization as follows:

1. The hospital's statement of its *mission, vision, and values* is created by the board of directors and/or senior leaders to articulate the hospital's values and direction. Mission and vision may change with time, but they usually guide the organization for many years. Values, however, are constant and do not change.
2. The hospital's *strategic plan* is created by senior administration and the board of trustees on an annual basis to establish overall strategies, objectives, and tactics for the organization. Usually, strategies are shared throughout all levels of the organization. Hospital strategies tend to be broad, and they affect the entire organization.
3. The annual *nursing services strategic plan* is sponsored by senior nursing leaders with input from middle managers to establish nursing

strategies. These strategies are derived from and must complement the hospital's overall strategies. The primary purpose of the nursing strategic plan is to identify the focus of nursing for the next year. A strategic plan helps to prioritize what is important to nursing. As a result, staff members are clear on what the nursing service expects to accomplish. Specific objectives should be focused, achievable, and measurable. Each nursing unit is expected to implement these objectives.

4. *Nursing unit goals and objectives,* revised annually, establish how the nursing unit will assist in implementing the nursing service strategies. Goals are broad statements of what will be accomplished; objectives the specific tactics of how to accomplish those goals. Unit goals and objectives should be focused, achievable, and measurable. If specific objectives for nursing units are developed as part of the nursing strategic plan, the nurse manager's role is to ensure that they are carried out. If there is no nursing strategic plan, unit goals and objectives must be derived from the hospital plan.

5. *Standards of performance* delineate key job responsibilities for a classification of personnel (for example, registered nurse) against which actual performance is measured. These criteria-based standards of performance are generic and usually identified for each registered nurse responsibility in the job description. They are not specific to unit goals but are important in assisting all registered nurses in knowing what is expected of them.

6. *Individual objectives* are established annually by staff members and their managers and outline very specifically how each individual staff member will assist in implementing unit goals and comply with standards of performance. Individual performance objectives may be established for the staff as part of what is expected during the upcoming appraisal year.

In many hospitals, the entire strategic plan is revised annually and serves as a blueprint for what is to be accomplished throughout the organization. The strategic planning process begins with broad statements describing general directions. As the process spreads through all levels of the organization, the goals, objectives, and tactics become more specific (see figure 3-5).

Some hospitals do not have a specific nursing strategic plan. In this case, the unit-based goals should be compatible with the hospital plan. Even when there is no hospital strategic plan, it is appropriate to develop unit-based goals and objectives to serve as the blueprint for the unit's strategic direction. To build a high-performance team, common goals and a sense of direction are essential.

Figure 3-5.   Example of a Strategic Planning Flow

Hospital Strategy:	Reduce cost per patient day by 5%
Nursing Strategy:	Increase non-RN skill mix and create RN/ancillary care teams
Unit Goal:	Convert three RN positions to five ancillary positions
Unit Objectives:	Contact human resources and complete conversion of RN position by (date); responsibility: manager
	All RNs will attend delegation seminar by (date); responsibility: manager
Individual Performance Objective:	Serves as preceptor to ancillary care team members

The following is an example of how unit-based goals are derived from a hospital strategic plan (when a nursing strategic plan is not available):

The hospital strategy is to develop a "center of excellence" in oncology. The nurse manager of oncology and her staff have a golden opportunity to develop synergistic goals that will benefit the hospital. Possible goals include:

- Staff will be certified in the nursing chemotherapy course within six months of hire.
- Family support groups will be held monthly and conducted by staff.
- Patient satisfaction will be at or above national norm.

Staff members should be actively involved in establishing unit goals and objectives. Objectives delineate specifically how the goals will be accomplished. Change is slow. Therefore, to ensure success, it is better to focus efforts on a few (no more than five) key goals. A feeling of ownership is also crucial to successful goal attainment. Furthermore, goals jointly prepared by the staff and managers will be more successful than goals that are mandated by managers. Progress should be monitored and successes celebrated.

How Can Participative Management Foster High Performance?

The nurse manager plays a pivotal role in creating a high-performance team. In order to be effective, the nurse manager must involve his or her staff in decision making at the unit level. Participation in decision making helps staff members grow and develop professionally. The following sections present some strategies the nurse manager can use in fostering team culture and encouraging team building.

Create a Team Culture

The nurse manager can stimulate team culture through utilizing the following management strategies:[1]

- *Be flexible.* Flexibility allows for freedom to try new ideas and keeps the number of rules, policies, and procedures to a minimum. On a nursing unit, employing creative scheduling techniques is one way the manager can demonstrate flexibility. Allowing staff to try new ideas should be fostered and encouraged.
- *Delegate responsibility.* Delegation of responsibility provides staff with the appropriate authority to get the job done. Staff must have the authority to talk with physicians, ancillary departments, and other professionals. In addition, staff must have the clout to get things done for patients. To ensure that staff has responsibility and authority, nurse managers must regularly follow up with those managers or departments not responsive to the needs brought forward by staff.
- *Establish clear standards.* Staff want to know that their manager and nursing service administrator are committed to quality and high performance.
- *Provide rewards.* Praise, recognition, and compensation commensurate with experience should be integral components of unit management.
- *Be clear.* Clarity involves open and accurate communication. Feedback should be ongoing and constant. Questions should be encouraged and answers provided.
- *Encourage commitment.* Staff should feel pride and ownership in the unit. Commitment is the key to staff retention and is possible only in an environment that empowers staff. This is done through shared decision making, consensus building, teamwork, and staff recognition.

A nurse manager enhances team culture by demonstrating the following attributes on a day-to-day basis:

- Acts as coach, counselor, and mentor to staff by enabling them to solve their own problems and accept progressive responsibility
- Provides clear direction, goals, and feedback on an ongoing basis
- Provides an environment open to risk taking and the implementation of new ideas, where innovation and creativity are fostered through positive reinforcement
- Acts as a role model demonstrating professional behavior
- Provides staff with appropriate clinical resources to enhance clinical expertise

- Encourages conflict resolution and negotiation among staff members and acts as arbitrator only when necessary
- Communicates openly and listens actively
- Serves as a team player in interactions with other hospital departments

Build the Team

Team building is a method of participative management that encourages staff commitment to the unit and the organization. Before trying to improve team performance, managers should first assess how the staff is functioning currently. A staff in need of team building may have inadequate conflict resolution skills, demonstrate low morale, bicker among themselves, and/or demonstrate little team interaction. Managers may also observe low scores on employee satisfaction results or high staff turnover and vacancy rates. The way staff members interact with each other and the nurse manager provides the most valuable indicator of whether team building is needed.

Steps a nurse manager may employ to facilitate team building include the following:

1. Assess team functioning through observations, interviews, feedback from other departments, cultural assessments, turnover rates, and exit interview data.
2. Look for symptoms of team dysfunction, including lack of teamwork, overuse of incident reports, poorly performing committees, lack of focus on patients, scapegoating, negativism, tunnel vision, lack of commitment, and disengagement.
3. Review data and analyze team strengths and weaknesses.
4. Develop team-building strategies, utilizing expertise from human resources, if needed.
5. Implement developed team-building strategies.
6. Evaluate the success of the team-building effort.

When assessing team functioning, managers should ask staff questions that focus on relationships and unit functioning. Individual interviews with each staff member will allow the managers to probe for further information or clarification when answers are unclear. Open-ended questions are recommended because they provide insight into team relationship problems. The manager should not assume that he or she knows what issues concern the staff. Questions to staff may include the following:

- Describe the way the unit functions in terms of teamwork.
- Describe the way the unit functions in terms of times of day (morning, evening, night).

- Describe relationships among shifts.
- Are there any cliques on the unit that affect teamwork negatively?
- How would you describe the morale of the unit?
- How are staff conflicts handled? Who solves them?
- What do you think the role of the manager should be in staff conflicts?
- What are the unit's strengths?
- What are the unit's weaknesses?
- What three things would you like to see changed on the unit?

After interviewing each staff member, the nurse manager reviews his or her notes and identifies common problems. Some of the most common problems that require team building include:

- Lack of conflict resolution skills among staff members
- Lack of team effort—individual work, not teamwork, being the norm
- High turnover
- Major communication problems among shifts
- Low morale among staff
- Informal clique on any shift that is viewed as negative and intimidating
- Expectation that the manager will solve all problems
- Lack of delegation to ancillary staff, resulting in overload for the registered nurses and frustration for the ancillary staff

A very effective way for a nurse manager to begin team building is to ask for staff volunteers from all shifts to work together to resolve a particular issue. One issue, for example, could be improving communication among shifts. The task force would be asked to compile and present its recommendations to the entire staff. Managers need to provide guidance to the task force, especially if it is the staff's first attempt at resolving an issue in this manner. The manager encourages active listening and brainstorming and rewards the group with positive feedback as they progress. The manager also requires that the task force achieve consensus among staff members before implementing recommendations. It is very important that the manager coaches staff from the beginning to the end of each project.

On topics such as conflict resolution, negotiation, and communication, the nurse manager may follow up one-on-one or suggest more formal education for staff. However, it is important to use and reward these techniques on a day-to-day basis. One way the manager can open up dialogue and move the team forward is to have staff develop expectations for the manager's role. The manager can also develop and share his or her expectations of the unit staff. As always, negotiation is key and the expectations must be realistic.

Building a team takes time and patience. Building a high-performance team is predicated on the staff members' ability to work together synergistically. Irregardless of high-performing individuals, building a high-performance team is not possible if team relationships are dysfunctional.

The success of team-building efforts can be evaluated through the following measures:

- Results of a cultural assessment, if available, may indicate improvement or lack of progress.
- Results of patient satisfaction surveys may show improvement or lack or progress.
- Letters of commendation or letters of complaint may be written to administration about the unit team from patients, families, or other departments.
- Morale may appear higher than before the project or show little change.
- Staff turnover may decrease or stay the same.
- Interviews with staff may show perceived improvement of team functioning or perceived lack of improvement.

Case Study: Building a Team

A newly appointed nurse manager knew that the challenges she faced on a 29-bed medical unit were formidable. Problems she had been told about during the interview process included:

- High turnover of staff (43 percent)
- Previous autocratic leadership
- Staff members functioning as individuals, not as a team
- Dissatisfied customers – physicians and patients
- Core of negative staff members functioned as the unit's informal leaders

Identify the Problems

The manager's first few days on the unit confirmed that there were serious problems and little team functioning. She conducted individual interviews with staff members and key admitting physicians. By asking open-ended questions, the new nurse manager was able to gain additional insight into the unit's problems. She reviewed exit interview data and employee opinion survey results, as well as observing interactions. In order to obtain a thorough understanding of the team's problems, she assessed its functioning for three months, after which she analyzed the information she had gathered.

The following problems were identified:

- Poor communication skills among nurses
- Inability of staff to confront each other about problems

- Manager as sole problem solver
- Bickering and fingerpointing among shifts
- Negativism among staff led by two specific people
- Favoritism in terms of work scheduling shown to two staff members

Identify Strategies

A strategy was developed for team building among staff members. The manager let the staff know what her expectations were and asked them to list collectively their expectations of the manager. This task, which was difficult for the staff, took almost two months to complete. However, open dialogue occurred among staff members for the first time. The staff's expectations of the manager were the following:

- Manager will demonstrate her support to staff by making daily rounds, holding regular staff meetings, and helping with problems.
- Manager will communicate fair expectations of all staff members.
- Manager will assist staff in dealing with difficult situations with patients, families, and physicians.
- Manager will allow staff to participate in clinical decisions at the unit level.

The manager discussed these expectations with staff and agreed that they were reasonable. The manager then presented the staff with her expectations:

- Staff will solve problems with each other and at least attempt resolution before involving the manager.
- Staff will negotiate changes in schedules with each other, involving the manager only as a last resort.
- Staff will work together to establish consistent unit guidelines for vacation, rotations, and coverage.
- Staff will identify educational needs and commit to attending inservices, as well as engaging in self-study.

Results

The dialogue was very beneficial in starting the team-building process. Scheduling was done consistently and fairly, resulting in the resignation of one staff member who refused to work nights. Staff expressed great relief over the resignation because that individual had a negative attitude and was intimidating to the staff.

As a team atmosphere began to develop, peer pressure forced a second nurse to change her negative behavior. Positive letters from patients began coming in to the unit, and the addition of staff helped to resolve the frustration of being short-staffed.

Volunteers from days and evenings worked together on a change-of-shift report that enhanced communication markedly. Staff members identified three educational needs on which inservice forums were then held—assertiveness, negotiation, and conflict resolution. Staff worked together on self-scheduling. Scheduling parameters were established and communicated to all staff, and all requests went through a newly created scheduling committee composed of six staff volunteers from all three shifts.

The process took over a year, but the end result was a stable, high-performing team that was recognized as one of the best units in the hospital.

Reward Behavior

Employees are motivated by rewards. Rewards can be external, such as praise, salary, or added responsibility. Other rewards are internal—the satisfaction of a job well done, for example. Rewarding behavior is a basic concept utilized every day in almost all situations. Designing creative rewards to reinforce behavior is a challenge, especially in this time of diminishing resources.

The first step in rewarding behavior starts with the nurse manager comparing the preset criteria-based performance appraisal with the employee's actual behavior. Figure 3-6 is a performance appraisal based on one element of the job description in figure 3-4. It is designed to weight the components of the job's various expectations. Assessment of patients is weighted at 35 percent of the expectation as a whole. Practitioners, therefore, know that 35 percent of their total evaluation points will be derived from this category. By combining objectives and performance

Figure 3-6. Example of a Performance Appraisal

Assessment of Patients

35% Demonstrates the ability to appropriately assess patients in a systematic way in order to promote optimal level of wellness. Documents patient assessment and teaching needs.

   6% Assesses patients in a systematic way and documents appropriately.

   5% Interviews and obtains patient history utilizing direct and indirect sources of data.

   4% Formulates nursing diagnoses through the identification of the patients' nursing problems.

   5% Identifies learning needs of patients and families.

   5% Identifies potential/actual discharge needs.

   4% Initiates referrals to the health care team.

   6% Identifies changes in the patient's condition and takes appropriate actions.

appraisal behavior tools, the manager can accurately assess the practitioner's performance. If warranted, a positive assessment can then be translated into a reward, such as a salary increase.

The performance appraisal not only describes tasks, but also values. Including value measurement in the performance evaluation tool is a relatively new concept that has helped managers more accurately assess the true worth of individuals on the unit. There is always a sense that some nurses are more valuable than others. By adding values to the performance assessment, the manager is able to determine how much an individual supports the values of the institution.

The nurse manager should identify specific behaviors when evaluating values. For example, a nurse might demonstrate positive behavior in the area of patient respect by addressing patients by their names. As another example, a nurse might adjust her personal schedule to accommodate a coworker's scheduling needs.

Because rewards are used to reinforce behavior, they should be positive in nature and viewed by the employee as something good. This may seem obvious, but it is possible that what one employee might see as a reward, another might not. For example, tuition reimbursement is not a very good reward for a staff member who is not motivated toward continuing education. For this reason, it is important that the nurse manager stay in tune with what the staff wants when the rewards are being designed.

There are other opportunities to recognize individual staff members. Specific behaviors can be rewarded through merit salary increases or cash bonuses. In addition, the use of cash-equivalent awards, such as scholarships and gift certificates, may also be effective.

There is enormous opportunity to recognize individuals with nonfinancial rewards carefully designed with both the institution and the individual in mind. Nonfinancial rewards might include a preferential schedule, assignment, or special added responsibilities.

Because patient satisfaction with nursing care can have a positive impact on the nurse's self-esteem, positive feedback from patients can also significantly motivate and reward staff. Therefore, it is important for the manager to provide mechanisms that facilitate patient feedback (for example, sending questionnaires to patients).

A more specific example of a patient feedback strategy is one that has been implemented through the SPIRIT program at Lutheran General Hospital in Park Ridge, Illinois. Patients, families, and staff members recognize each other by sending, through a formalized system, simple, easy messages directly to the administration. There are note cards and drop-off points throughout the hospital. Approximately 500 quick thank-yous per month go directly to employees and supervisors. This program has been an enormous source of pride to employees who wear the pins that commemorate such thank-yous. Staff can also be rewarded and recognized by identifying their contributions through the use of bulletin boards and/or a unit staff newsletter.

Units also may be rewarded. Recognizing unit-based team spirit and synergy on a formal basis can be effective. Criteria should be clearly defined, and the units should be evaluated against the criteria. The reward can take the form of official announcements of accomplishment or cash to fulfill a particular unit need (for example, a reference book, an outside speaker, or a new piece of equipment). Other ways of recognizing unit performance could be implementing a nurse-of-the-month program, recognizing a special nursing contribution or project, or hosting unit recognition breakfasts, lunches, or dinners.

☐ Retaining Successful Practitioners

Recruiting staff is not only expensive, but disruptive to the unit culture. Although it is difficult to quantify the cost of recruiting new nurses, the tangible costs include:

- Advertising
- Human resource time to interview candidates
- Manager time to interview candidates
- Staff development time to train new hires
- Unit staff time to orient new hires
- Interim replacement staff for open positions

A significant but intangible cost may result from lower staff morale at having to "take up the slack" until new staff is oriented and ready to assume full responsibility. Recruiting and orienting new staff may take several weeks to several months. Therefore, no matter how good the recruiting process, it is much more cost-effective to retain staff.

The nurse manager's retention efforts should be directed at maintaining the satisfaction of the "right" people on staff, those who will create a high-performance team. For example, if the staff values higher education, the manager might want to include some job incentive by adding tuition reimbursement after two years of employment. That strategy will not please all of the staff, because there will be some individuals who have no interest in continuing education. However, if the institution-at-large values continuing education, it will be a retention motivator to the nurses whom the manager most values.

The best way to maximize retention efforts is through the use of interdisciplinary teams. These groups assess what motivates staff and determine how to provide rewards at the unit and at the hospital level to ensure retention of high-performance employees. The interdisciplinary teams can be hospital or unit based.

How Are Hospitalwide Retention Teams Organized?

Hospitalwide retention issues should also be addressed by a multidisciplinary team. The team should include:

- Nursing leaders and staff
- Human resource personnel (representing compensation, benefits, and employee relations)
- A financial analyst
- A marketing representative
- A nurse recruiter

Each team member brings specific skills to the committee. For example, nursing leaders and staff can help assess just how severe the turnover problem is. Human resource personnel are aware of competitors' offerings in salary and benefits. Through employee exit interviews, they understand, in more detail, previous employees' problems and dissatisfactions

Many hospitals also periodically conduct sessions to solicit employee feedback about various issues, including benefits, salary, work load, and work environment. This type of feedback is critical to the success of the retention committee's work. The marketing department can conduct focus groups to learn what nurses want. In addition, marketing can provide valuable research about the nurse population demographics, identifying what that group wants.

One of the hospitalwide retention team's objectives might be to reduce nurse turnover to an acceptable 10 percent. The team might accomplish this by:

- Instituting a clinical ladder designed to satisfy nurses' need to advance clinically
- Creating an incentive task force to look at cash incentives for various staffing shortages
- Implementing a creative scheduling task force enabling mothers to work while their children are at school
- Increasing benefits for individuals who stay, such as graduated tuition reimbursement based on tenure

Salary and benefits are not the only, nor are they always the most effective, methods of retention. Only through careful analysis will the staff and its needs be revealed. The retention task force should assess these needs and make appropriate recommendations to management. These strategies should become part of the nursing strategic plan.

Turnover rates traditionally measure the success of a nursing retention program. However, there are some concerns with turnover reports. Some people leave for reasons beyond the control of any retention program. In addition, nursing is a traditionally transient industry. A meaningful turnover report would compare turnover rates with those of other units in the hospital. The hospital might also evaluate its turnover by comparing its rate with other similar hospitals.

How Are Unit-Level Retention Teams Organized?

On the unit level, successful retention planning and implementation include organizing an interdisciplinary team inclusive of staff, managers, resources personnel, and financial analysts. An example of one unit's approach to solving what it saw as a retention problem follows.

Case Study: Organizing a Team
The clinical manager of a six-bed postoperative cardiovascular unit convened a group of staff members to work on a short-term task force to come up with a solution to the staffing issues. The manager reviewed the following facts:

- There had been a 38 percent turnover in the past two years. (Hospital average turnover was 15 percent.)
- The current staff was frustrated with habitually having to work overtime because of staff shortages. Routinely, the staff members were staying long after their scheduled hours in order to complete their charting and care.
- The staff was feeling typical symptoms of burnout, including fatigue, anxiety, and sleeplessness.

The manager asked the group to brainstorm about what their specific problems were. The group came up with a long list that was synthesized into the following:

- Morale was very low due to the high-acuity patient case load and shortage of staff.
- There was too much work to get done in an eight-hour shift.
- The staff needed more time away from the acutely ill patients to be effective when they were with them.

The manager charged the group with coming up with a strategy that would help solve the staff turnover problem. The group determined that the problem related to the severity of illness on the unit. They felt that they could care better for their patients if allowed to care for these patients for longer stretches of time. Better care also involved them having more time away from the unit to rest.

The group decided on a plan to move the staff to 12-hour shifts and have only two shifts per day. They determined that this approach would work in their area because they had equal numbers of staff on days and nights. Assistance was sought from the finance department to help quantify the added salary expense. Next, they went back to the clinical manager and showed how the change would affect the unit schedule and how they proposed to fill the scheduling vacancies left by the conversion. The manager decided that in order to offset the salary expense, overtime and call-in help had to be minimized. She agreed to adopt the plan on a three-month trial basis, after which time outcomes would be measured.

At the end of the three months, overtime and on-call help was measured and found to have dropped from 40 to 2 hours per pay period. There had been no staff turnover during the trial period. Staff satisfaction surveys gave the program an A++. The clinical manager recommended to administration that the program be instituted in her unit on a permanent basis.

This retention project worked on this unit because of the following circumstances:

- The manager sponsored the problem-solving efforts.
- The manager involved the staff.
- The basic cause of the problem was identified.
- The staff came up with the solution.
- The solution fit the problem, not the symptoms.
- The measurements of the program's success were concrete.

☐ Improving Work Processes

Whereas the appropriate culture and the right people are the first two components in creating a high-performance team, process improvement is an important third. Work processes create the underlying structure of activity on the unit. There are hundreds of processes that staff follow on the unit. Some are automatic and straightforward, and others are so complicated and occasional that the individual must consult the procedure manual to accomplish them. However, processes are the backbone of all work that is done. It is the manager's job to design processes in such a way that staff are able to accomplish their tasks successfully and in doing so achieve high-quality outcomes.

Because processes underlie all unit activities, those that do not work well or fail to fully optimize resources hinder high performance. Managers must constantly evaluate the processes implemented on the unit, always looking for possible improvements and correcting those that are not successful. Correcting processes that are not working well is best accomplished by using a team approach. The team should include both managers and staff members who are intimately involved in the process or processes being examined.

As illustrated in the case study presented later in this chapter, many hospitals have changed their approach to quality improvement. If there is a problem on a particular unit or throughout the institution, it is probably because there is something wrong with one or more processes, rather than with the people involved. This approach provides staff with the opportunity to solve problems by changing the way patient care is delivered.

The following strategies are essential to process improvement:

- Involving those people who are involved in the process being improved (this may include people from other units or disciplines)
- Defining the improvements sought
- Setting expectations for the improvement by which success will be measured
- Being sure that staff is in alignment with the goals
- Being committed to making the improvements

The people doing the work can describe the processes involved; however, they need management to help implement the improvements. For example, an improvement may require changing the staffing mix or the responsibilities of different job classifications.

The role of the clinical manager is to coach staff and enable them to improve processes. Blaming and finding fault are inconsistent with improving processes. Some staff members will need coaching and education to help them perform at optimal levels. However, the great majority of problems affecting quality of care and high performance are related to processes. It is management's role to make those processes simple and correct so that staff are able to accomplish their tasks accurately and efficiently.

Case Study: Improving a Process

History

The quality assurance department in hospital X found a particular unit delinquent in preparing patient care plans. The institutional standard was that all patients will have care plans by the second day of hospitalization.

In reading the quality assurance report, the clinical manager discovered that her unit had a higher percentage of patients without patient care plans on day two than did her peers' units.

Old Quality Assurance Approach

The clinical manager called a staff meeting. She told the staff that they would all complete care plans on their patients by the second day and that she would be doing random checks on the charts to make sure that the plans were there. Two weeks later, the rate had improved and she felt much better. However, she was disappointed when the problem re-emerged a month later.

New Quality Improvement Approach

The clinical manager called a meeting to ask staff why they were unable to complete the care plans as requested. The staff responded that the patients came to their unit from the ICU, where they had care plans already in place. The staff also said that they did not use a care plan format for any part of the day-to-day care. The clinical manager and staff then brainstormed and came up with several ideas. They decided to utilize the care plan initiated in the ICU and add to it, rather than starting a new one. The staff and manager also decided to use the care plan as a reporting document at change of shift. They agreed that evaluation of the proposed solution would be based on staff compliance. As staff compliance was monitored, it was noted that patients, at first, had completed care plans 75 percent of the time. Compliance increased, however, over subsequent monitoring checks.

The rationale for this approach came out of the following perspectives or attitudes: Staff are intrinsically motivated to do what is expected of them. If they are not complying with expectations, something is preventing compliance. The clinical manager knew that the staff understood the unit processes better than she did. Staff knew they were free to state the situational problems without fear of censure. Thus, the manager helped staff solve the problem, rather than solving it for them. Furthermore, using the care plan started in another area was a way of recognizing the unit as a part of a whole system, not merely an isolated area. The solution implemented recognized that the problem involved process—not staff compliance. When the process was improved, compliance improved.

Evaluation Mechanisms

The success level of each process improvement project must be evaluated. Was what was set out to be done, accomplished? In this case study, the goal was to improve the compliance in care plan preparation. The group was careful not to set a particular compliance goal, but to work toward improvement, the assumption being that until compliance reaches 100 percent, there is always room for improvement. However, setting the goal at 100 percent might be discouraging and serve to demotivate, rather than motivate, staff. Therefore, the goal was to continually strive for better compliance.

□ Conclusion

It takes the appropriate culture, the right people, and the continuous improvement of processes to create a high-performance team. With a high-performance team, a highly motivated staff directs itself and the institution toward appropriate goals. It is the role of the manager to create the appropriate culture; to hire, motivate, and retain the right people; and to facilitate the creation of processes that will enable the staff to succeed. It is an enormous task but one of the most important in the institution. By creating an environment that encourages high performance and commitment to quality, nurse executives and nurse managers can make a significant difference in the way an institution functions.

□ *Reference*

1. Dubnick, C. Building high-performance management team. *Healthcare Forum Journal.* 34(3):24, May/June 1991.

☐ Chapter 4

Managing Stress among Nurses

Priscilla Lynch, M.S., R.N.,
and Susanne DeFabiis, M.S., R.N.

There are several definitions of stress and many perspectives from which to view the concept. In his classic definition, Selye identifies stress as "the nonspecific response of the body to any demand made on it."[1] Lazarus perceived stress as an interactive response between an individual and a stressor. He defines stress as "a situation in which environmental demands, internal demands, or both, tax or exceed the adaptive resources of an individual, social, or tissue system."[2]

However one defines it, stress is one of the most critical elements in nursing management. It can cause high turnover, poor patient care delivery, illness, and over time, high vacancy rates. Although stress is inherent in the nursing profession, nurse executives and nurse managers can use certain techniques to reduce stress among staff. Reducing stress can resolve conflicts in the workplace. It can decrease absenteeism, feelings of demoralization and rigidity, interpersonal and interdisciplinary conflicts, and high turnover rates. Reducing stress can also increase the quality of patient care delivery and enhance nurse satisfaction.

This chapter examines the nature of stress in relation to professional nursing and provides insight into and practical management strategies for dealing with stress within an organization. The text is divided into two sections. The first defines how stress occurs and affects individuals. Being aware of stress processes can help nurse managers to assess and recognize current and potential staff problems. Understanding the stress process and where problems exist will guide nurse managers in solving those problems.

The second section describes specific strategies for eliminating or reducing harmful stress. All strategies do not alleviate all types of stress. It is important to identify the source of harmful stress *before* choosing an appropriate strategy to eliminate it. Therefore, this section will identify the sources of the stress before describing appropriate strategies.

☐ The Stress Process

Stress is a process—a series of events and reactions that individuals experience in the course of day-to-day living. Although there are many different interpretations and explanations of the stress process this chapter focuses mainly on theories from the work of Richard Lazarus whose framework was chosen because it "views the psychological response to stress as a transactional phenomenon. This transactional view of stress implies that not only does the environment affect the person but also that the person affects the environment."[3] This view is applicable to the nursing environment. The process may be perceived as consisting of four phases:

1. *Stressors*—Individuals come into contact with stressors.
2. *Primary appraisals*—Individuals perceive the stressors as harmful or benign.
3. *Secondary appraisals (coping)*—Individuals make attempts to cope with the stressors.
4. *Outcomes*—Individuals effectively or ineffectively cope, which may lead to enhanced growth or illness.

Stressors

Stressors are situations or life events that create pressure or stress within an individual. There are three different types of stressors:

- Physical
- Psychological
- Social

Physical stressors are biological or physical insults to the body (for example, infections, poisoning, and extreme temperature changes). Psychological stressors are emotional situations (for example, deaths in the family, job losses, and interpersonal conflicts). Social stressors are societal changes or problems (for example, prejudice, war, and poverty).

Stressors are neither negative nor positive in themselves. How the individual reacts to the stressor determines whether it will cause eustress (positive stress—associated with pleasant effects) or distress (negative stress—associated with unpleasant effects). Eustress is a vital ingredient of life and is necessary for an individual's continued growth and survival. We need situations that will challenge, motivate, and stimulate us. Otherwise, we grow bored and fatigued with life. Distress often leads to confusion, frustration, and pain. It is the result of perceiving a stressor as harmful or threatening to an individual's sense of well-being.

Primary Appraisals

The second phase, *primary appraisal,* can be described as how individuals perceive and appraise stressors. The individual's subjective appraisal of an event triggers his or her response to the stressor involved. Stress, according to Lazarus, does not reside predominantly in the individual or in the event. It is the interaction between the two that defines an event as stressful.

Lazarus's model consists of two stages of assessment (or appraisal): primary and secondary.[4] The initial reaction to the potentially stressful situation is the primary appraisal. During this stage, individuals choose one of three viewpoints or perceptions regarding the stressful event:

• The event is harmful.
• The event is threatening.
• The event is challenging.

If individuals respond in one of the first two ways, they perceive the event as negatively stressful—and the feelings generated those of distress. Once an event is appraised as negatively stressful, a secondary appraisal is formulated. In this secondary appraisal, an individual decides what type of coping process he or she will utilize to deal with the particular stressful event. For example, the individual may choose to avoid the threat, display anger, or become fearful.

The following vignette illustrates this concept:

Ms. Smith, a nurse working in the special care nursery, has recently completed her orientation. She is approached by her preceptor, who states, "Today, I asked the charge nurse if she would change your assignment so that you can care for only one very complicated case."

Ms. Smith wants to prove her competence. She leaves this interaction feeling that her preceptor lacks confidence in her abilities and, therefore, has arranged for her to take care of only one patient. On the other hand, the preceptor walks away from this interaction feeling that she has lightened Ms. Smith's patient load, decreased her anxiety, and given her an opportunity to care for a complicated patient. The preceptor feels that by focusing exclusively on learning all aspects of one very complicated case, Ms. Smith will feel an enhanced sense of competence.

At noon Ms. Smith skips lunch. The nurse manager finds her crying in the nurses' lounge. The nurse manager takes Ms. Smith to her office to talk. Ms. Smith reveals that she feels that her preceptor perceives her as inadequate and wonders whether she should continue working in the special care nursery.

Here, in the primary appraisal, both the nurse graduate and the preceptor perceive the situation as stressful. The preceptor attempted to lighten the patient load for the new nurse and encourage her to perceive the situation as a challenge. However, the new nurse perceived the preceptor's actions as yet another stressful event and as harmful, not challenging.

Secondary Appraisals

The third phase, *secondary appraisal,* is how individuals attempt to eliminate painful stress. This can be accomplished by utilizing coping strategies and enhancing inner resilience.

Coping

Individuals use certain strategies, or coping mechanisms, to help them deal with stressful events. Lazarus defines *coping* as:

> A process characterized by continuous use of goal directed strategies that are initiated and maintained over time and across encounters by means of cognitive appraisal and regulating emotional and physiological responses.[5]

Coping strategies include denial, confrontation, and avoidance. Sometimes these strategies are useful; other times they are detrimental. Individuals choose strategies that will minimize pain. The ideal outcome of a positive coping strategy is that the individual masters the situation and enhances his or her personal integrity. All coping mechanisms can be seen across a continuum. Sometimes the mechanisms can help an individual to better assess and then deal with the stressful situation. At other times, coping mechanisms can interfere or block an individual's insight. For example, a nurse taking care of a diabetic patient who is noncompliant in learning to self-inject insulin may support this dependency by continually doing the task for the patient. The nurse's action may be temporary until he or she can develop a better strategy to help the patient overcome his or her noncompliant stance, or it may be the nurse's way of dealing with his or her own need to be nurturing and competent. It is important that nurses develop an awareness of the strategies they use when interacting with patients.

Resilience

Resilience is an inner quality that appears to strengthen the individual's ability to cope. Flach defines resilience as "the psychological and biological strengths required to successfully master change."[6] Characteristics specific to resilience include:[7]

- Having a strong, durable sense of self-esteem
- Being able to compromise in interpersonal relationships
- Maintaining a well-established network of personal friends, including one or more who serve as confidants
- Having a high level of personal discipline and a sense of responsibility
- Recognizing and developing one's own special gifts and talents
- Being open-minded and receptive to new ideas
- Being capable of dreaming
- Having a wide range of interests
- Maintaining a keen sense of humor
- Having a high distress tolerance
- Being committed to life and a philosophical framework in which personal experiences are interpreted with meaning and hope
- Thinking and acting independently without fearing or relying on others
- Having insight into one's own feelings as well as those of others, and having the ability to communicate one's feelings in an appropriate manner

Outcomes

Whatever the stressful event and however an individual reacts to it, there will be an outcome. An individual can grow from the event, return to a previous level of functioning, or regress. The first two outcomes can lead to more effective coping. The first option helps an individual to master the situation. The second helps an individual to return to a level of comfort in his or her interactions with the environment. On the other hand, the third outcome, regression, leads to ineffective coping and often physical breakdown or disease.

Burnout in nursing is an example of a distress/disease situation. It is often produced by ineffective attempts to cope with the many occupational stresses found within the nursing profession. McCarthy defines *burnout* as:

> A progressive physical and emotional exhaustion involving the development of negative job attitudes and perceptions, and a loss of empathic concern for the patients. It is caused by chronic stress resulting from a prolonged intensive involvement with people.[8]

Burnout carries a high cost for individuals, coworkers, and health services in general. Burned-out nurses experience emotional, attitudinal, medical, and family problems. Nurses' coworkers respond to the stress of others by exhibiting lower morale and providing less-effective care. Finally, the institution is affected. It delivers a poorer quality of care and experiences high levels of turnover and absenteeism.

The early symptoms of burnout are emotional and physical exhaustion, fatigue, insomnia, and susceptibility to minor illnesses. Other symptoms of burnout include feelings of hopelessness, helplessness, and entrapment. Burned-out nurses also develop a negative self-image and negative attitudes toward work, life, and other people. This cynicism leads to the final symptom—total disgust with everyone and everything. Storlie states that "burnout is resignation to a lack of power, the perception that no matter what you do or how hard you try, you cannot make a difference in the situation."[9]

☐ Intervention in the Stress Process

By first identifying the negative stressors and then intervening to eliminate them, nurse managers can effectively maneuver the stress process to maximize growth and minimize stagnation. Nurse managers can intervene in the stress process by identifying and removing negative stressors, enhancing positive perceptions of stressors, and encouraging healthy coping mechanisms and resilience.

Identify and Remove Negative Stressors

The more stressors in the environment, the higher the dissatisfaction is among nurses. Eliminating negative stressors can increase the probability of healthy outcomes. For example, a unit that lacks adequate supplies is subject to a negative stressor. Providing the supplies eliminates a specific negative stressor and decreases the overall stress. Therefore, there is a higher probability that the nurses will be satisfied.

Methods for Identifying Negative Stressors

Nurse managers identify negative stressors by sharing information and perceptions with staff and other health care professionals, observing what is occurring on the unit or in the department, and evaluating patient care complaints. Information can be obtained through staff meetings, interdepartmental meetings, and suggestion boxes. If the entire staff is responding to a stressor, the nurse manager should plan a meeting and ask staff members to identify the problem and suggest possible solutions. If only one staff member is responding to a stressor, the nurse manager should plan a one-on-one meeting. Surveying patients also provides the nurse manager valuable information. In addition, managers can identify negative stressors during the formal staff evaluation process.

Gribbons and Marshall identify the following common categories of negative stressors:[10]

- *Nursing tasks*—the number, frequency, and complexity of tasks
- *Workload*—the complex patient care required for higher-acuity patients (it is important to measure workload accurately when allocating patient assignments)
- *Death and dying*—the frequency of dealing with death and dying issues can be very stressful (communicating bad news to patients and families)
- *Uncertainty*—the fact that the corporate culture of health care is constantly changing and that many decisions are made with little nursing input
- *Responsibility*—the combination of higher technology, sicker patients, and fewer resources that requires nurses to increase their levels of responsibility and independent decision making
- *Role conflict*—the requirement that nurses, as well as being high-tech caregivers, be all things to all people (in addition, many nurses live with high internal expectations that can often leave them feeling unsettled and frustrated)
- *Relationships with patients, relatives of patients, physicians, and colleagues*— the constant expectation that nurses function as communicators and coordinators
- *Work–home conflicts*—the demands of work and home mixed with personal expectations of being highly successful in both areas
- *Other expectations of nurse roles*—the expectations of society, patients, coworkers combined to leave nurses feeling as though they are failures when they do not meet every expectation

Strategies for Removing Negative Stressors

Once the stressors have been identified, a process should be put into place for coping with them. Following are some management strategies for eliminating or reducing negative stressors. Awareness of negative stressors and their potential impact on the nursing environment should enable nurse managers to utilize these strategies proactively.

Creative Scheduling
Scheduling difficulties can be one of the most pervasive problems for managers as well as staff. When the nurse manager involves staff nurses in the scheduling process, they feel a sense of ownership and accountability. Flexibility with 4-, 8-, 10-, 12-hour shifts can meet a large number

of needs. Allowing for full-time, part-time, float-pool, and job-sharing positions can reduce negative stressors. Creative scheduling may also help alleviate shortages by pulling nurses who may find full-time work unacceptable back into the work force. Encouraging staff to participate in decision making will ensure that the manager is addressing the appropriate stressors, such as uncertainty, role conflict, powerlessness, and lack of control.

Restructuring

To eliminate nurse task and work load stressors, nurse managers and staff may want to identify and implement a different patient care delivery system. Being able to utilize nurse assistants to perform tasks that consume large amounts of nursing time can help relieve the nurses' work load and sense of frustration. (See chapter 5 for a more in-depth discussion of this strategy.)

Adequate Registered Nurse/Patient Ratio

Ensuring adequate staffing can reduce negative stressors. Although this factor cannot always be controlled by the nurse manager, promoting a unit environment of openness and acceptance encourages the sharing of future plans, including terminations. In an open environment it should be easier for the nurse manager to provide adequate staff to meet the patient work load. The nurse manager must also engage in responsible hiring by recruiting appropriate applicants whose characteristics fit the specific unit environment. Also, during the probationary period for new staff, nurse managers can weed out potential competency problems that often lead to increased feelings of stress for experienced staff.

Educational Programs

Educational programs can help staff adapt to the constantly changing health care environment. One environmental stressor is the expectation for high technical performance. Stress is lessened for staff when they are educated and updated in technical areas. There are also educational programs that promote personal growth and development. These can help nurses look at their internal expectations more realistically. Educational programs can be as varied and creative as required to meet the staff's needs. A yearly (or even quarterly) staff needs assessment can assist nurse managers in deciding what educational programs would be beneficial. Nurse managers may want to utilize unit-based programs. However, they may find that department- or institution-based programs also meet some of their needs as well as conserve resources. Managers support educational programs by providing time for staff to attend.

New Products Committees

Involving staff nurses on a new products committee is another strategy managers can use to reduce stress. Staff members gain a sense of control over their practice and become more comfortable with the new equipment if they are allowed input in deciding which products will be purchased.

Greater Autonomy and Decision Making

Feeling a lack of control over what one does can be a source of frustration and stagnation. Nurse managers foster a staff's sense of confidence and commitment when they allow staff to develop a sense of autonomy in decision making. A nurse manager should encourage staff growth and development and allow staff the freedom to make mistakes. Such an environment enhances the staff's level of comfort in making patient care judgments.

Enhance Positive Perceptions of Stressors

An individual's perception of an event triggers that individual's response. This subsection focuses on how the nurse manager can help to reframe the perception of an event from negative to positive.

Methods for Identifying Negative Perceptions

Examples of negative perceptions nurses may have include feeling a lack of support from nurse administrators, a sense of not being an important member of the health care team, and a lack of control over the work environment. Nurse managers must be able to recognize those behaviors in order to identify underlying problems before they get out of hand. Negative perceptions, whether distorted or based on reality, have a significant effect on teamwork, morale, turnover rates, and the quality of patient care.

Nurse managers can identify negative perceptions—as reflected in cynicism, sarcasm among staff members, lack of patience with each other and with patients and their families, and a reluctance to help each other— during the normal workday and during staff meetings. Cues suggesting further assessment also include patient, family, and physician complaints. An ongoing unit advisory group that identifies issues and potential problems may also be helpful in combatting negative perceptions. The group should include staff nurses and nurse managers.

Strategies for Enhancing Positive Perceptions

Strategies to enhance positive perceptions of stressors may be directed at solving existing problems or preventing problems from occurring. Following are some strategies for enhancing adaptive coping.

Create a Culture of Opportunity

The unit culture should reflect a challenging, positive perception of the nursing profession wherein everyone has common goals and works as a team. It is imperative that all staff buy in to this philosophy. Nurse managers create a culture of opportunity by role modeling, fostering a professional practice environment, encouraging risk taking, and implementing discipline without punishment. Involving staff in management decisions is also helpful. The unit culture should provide opportunities for individuals to enhance self-esteem within the work group, thereby encouraging the perceptions of growth.

Promote Empowerment

Empowerment allows individuals to feel a sense of control over their work environment. Nurse managers promote staff empowerment by keeping staff abreast of information, changes, and issues concerning both the unit and the organization as a whole. Nurse managers who know the system can help staff work effectively within it. Nurse managers can also promote empowerment by involving the staff in unit decisions, establishing task forces to meet desired goals, and encouraging committee involvement in decision making.

Provide Educational Programs

By learning to reframe their perceptions of stressors, the staff becomes more adaptive at coping. Educational programs are useful tools for teaching such topics as creating a culture of opportunity, empowerment, creativity, autonomy, and conflict management; giving feedback; and enhancing individuals' self-esteem. For example, if team building is a problem in a unit, nurse managers may elect to offer an inservice program on how to be a better team member through enhancing communication skills.

The manager should choose a methodology that encourages staff to share ideas and thoughts. Sometimes learning can best take place during interactive programs, rather than through straight lectures. Oftentimes bringing in outside resources may also be helpful in educating the staff in specific areas.

Encourage Nurse–Physician Liaison Meetings

Nurse–physician liaison meetings help increase communication and prevent problems from arising or escalating. These meetings serve as interdisciplinary forums for identifying common goals and expectations. These forums also provide a framework for better understanding of roles.

Encourage Good News Swapping

As suggested by McBride, nurse managers should acknowledge staff and individual accomplishments. Managers can do this by verbally addressing individuals at staff meetings, pinning announcements on a unit bulletin board, or recognizing individuals in a unit or department newsletter. Positive feedback is an effective management strategy that creates a positive environment.[11]

Emphasize Outcomes

Nurse managers should identify specific outcomes and stick with them. The manager sets realistic goals for the unit or department and then provides support so that staff can work toward meeting them. Also, the manager organizes a celebration when the staff meets the goals. Meetings to assess whether deadlines have been met are important ways to evaluate goal accomplishments. These meetings should be held regularly throughout the year.[12]

Provide More Than Maintenance

Nurse managers help staff focus on activities that are future directed. In addition to annual goals, the manager and staff should discuss projected five-year goals and describe where the unit and/or department fits into the institution's future. Nurse managers should continually encourage staff to better themselves by helping them to identify personal goals and allowing them to participate in workshops and educational programs.[13]

Identify Research as an Activity of Hope

Participating in nursing research demonstrates the manager's commitment to the nursing profession. In addition, allowing staff to participate in these studies gives them more control over their environment and includes them in the problem-solving process. Often, staff may identify and develop a research protocol for addressing difficult issues. This activity enables them to utilize research outcomes to promote change within the unit and sometimes within the profession. The manager should encourage staff and give them time to participate in hospitalwide research projects and unit-based studies. Research should be identified as a legitimate staff function.[14]

Demonstrate Feelings of Optimism

It is important for a manager to emphasize and demonstrate positive attitudes. Specific strategies include these:

- Take care of yourself. How do you, as a manager, handle stress?
- Do the best you can. Don't expect to be perfect.
- No one is perfect. Don't expect others to be perfect or you will be disappointed.
- In order to succeed, expect occasional failure. It is through failure that important lessons are learned and success may be found.

- Break big jobs down into small components. Regard each completion as a success.
- Think situationally, not globally. Accomplishing many small things can equal a larger success overall.[15]

Be a Role Model

Nurse managers must look at their own behavior and make sure it is consistent with the organization's values and goals. Nurse managers also must be able to look at the way in which they assess situations and solve problems. At times, in order to deal with multifaceted demands, nurse managers may need to change their management techniques and behavior. The manager must develop a repertoire of management techniques appropriate to different situations. For example, sometimes the nurse manager might have to be firm and unbending, other times flexible and supportive. The key is to develop a sensitivity to the timeliness and effectiveness of different approaches.

Demonstrate Leadership Behaviors

When a nurse manager demonstrates certain leadership behaviors, positive perceptions of stressors can be enhanced. These behaviors include:

- *Awareness.* Are you able to pick up on minor issues before they become major? Small problems are easier to solve than large ones.
- *Availability.* How available are you? Does your level of availability meet your staff's needs?
- *Clinical expertise.* What are your clinical strengths and weaknesses? Are you comfortable letting staff know about them? Make staff aware of your strengths and weaknesses. Supplement your weaknesses with others' strengths.
- *Approachability.* How approachable are you? Is this communicated to staff? Staff members need to feel that they can come to you with their ideas and problems.
- *Environmental awareness.* Do you have your finger on the pulse of the institution? What are your system's nuances? Do you act as a buffer between the institution and the nursing staff?
- *Personal integrity.* How honest, self-aware, and confident are you? Are you considered fair, open, flexible, spontaneous? Would your staff identify these as your characteristics? Staff respects managers with strong personal integrity.

Stay Up-to-Date

New theories and research are being developed all the time. It is important for nurse managers to keep abreast of the latest management techniques and to promote continued self-growth and sensitivity within the organization. Attending professional conferences and small-group forums and reading professional literature are ways for nurse managers to develop these skills and acquire strategies for dealing with difficult staff problems. Utilizing these resources can also provide the nurse manager with a "hopeful perspective"–one in which the problems he or she encounters are not unique and solutions are available even for those situations that seem overwhelming.

☐ Encouraging Healthy Coping Mechanisms and Enhancing Resilience

Although everyone copes with stress in some way, each individual uses different strategies or coping mechanisms. However, unhealthy coping mechanisms lead to illness or burnout. Nurse managers can encourage staff to use healthy coping mechanisms. Staff resilience can be enhanced by first identifying negative coping mechanisms and then providing the support necessary to create a more positive environment.

Identify Maladaptive Coping Mechanisms

Initially, it is helpful for nurse managers to be able to differentiate maladaptive coping mechanisms from the more adaptive ones. By definition, maladaptive coping strategies create more problems. While some strategies may work in the short run, they will often fail in the long run. For example, after a stressful day, a nurse may have a few beers. As a one-time occurrence, this may help the nurse feel better and will probably have no negative side effects. However, if this strategy is used over time, its effects can be extremely detrimental.

Nurse managers can identify maladaptive coping strategies by being aware of staff members' behaviors. Signs of maladaptive coping behaviors include denial, fantasy or wishful thinking, emotional repression, rigidity, and use of aggressive versus assertive confrontational tactics. These maladaptive strategies can result in the following behavioral and emotional outcomes: anxiety, fear, distrust, forgetfulness, feelings of being overwhelmed, depression, panic, hopelessness, frustration, helplessness, powerlessness, and decreased self-esteem and self-confidence.

Encourage Healthy Coping Mechanisms

Nurse managers strive to help nursing staff utilize and develop healthy coping mechanisms. Adaptive coping strategies should both decrease feelings of burnout and increase feelings of support, giving staff members a greater sense of control over their environment. This subsection describes specific strategies for encouraging adaptive coping mechanisms and enhancing resilience.

Enhancing Social Support Systems

When staff members are allowed to build support systems and alliances within the work group, increased independent decision making and senses of self develop. Social support can be enhanced through informal and formal strategies.

Informal support strategies include:

- Scheduling regular staff meetings to provide informal forums and opportunities for staff and the nurse manager to discuss issues other than unit business. These issues may focus on the communication process between staff and administration, lack of staff motivation, or difficult patient situations. Consultation/liaison nurses are especially helpful in these arenas.
- Organizing an informal potluck meal to provide an opportunity for informal communication.
- Acknowledging staff anniversary dates with posters or even a baby photo contest to provide means for informal staff get togethers and communication.

Formal support strategies include:

- Organizing time-limited peer support groups that provide an opportunity to develop problem-solving techniques. These support groups can focus on a variety of issues (patient acuity or emotional issues of care giving, for example). Be careful to limit these groups both by time (sixty to ninety minutes for each meeting) and number of sessions (six to eight) because they tend to lose their effectiveness over time and can lead to negative, powerless gripe sessions. Consultation/liaison nurses can be helpful.
- Implementing a recognition and rewards program to encourage peer support and positive relationships. This program can be very creative and should address the specific needs of the staff. Staff can publish a newsletter identifying successes and accomplishments of nurses at all levels. Formal awards may be given for achievements in clinical practice, innovative ideas, or teamwork. Recognition and rewards celebrate the concept of success and encourage peer support.
- Creating nursing committees that have a hospitalwide, departmentwide, or unit-based focus. These committees bring nurses together in a forum and encourage them to become aware of other nursing

issues. These forums encourage nurses to work together toward a common goal.

- Organizing physician–nurse teams to provide a multidisciplinary approach to resolving real or potential conflicts.

Providing Opportunities for Exercise and Recreation Time

Exercise (either before work, during lunchtime, or after work) can be a positive way of bringing people together. Group exercise, for example, could be offered in the physical therapy room at the end of the day. Intramural activities (for example, volleyball, bowling) can also be organized. Providing these types of opportunities fosters camaraderie and enhances a sense of team spirit, which can lead to an increased sense of trust. People are often more open and spontaneous during these activities.

Confronting Situations Honestly and Openly

It is very easy for conflict to promote maladaptive coping strategies. Nurse managers can promote healthy strategies by allowing staff members to solve their own problems, with the manager providing support and intervention only as necessary. Staff members need to learn how to give feedback in a positive and assertive manner. The nurse manager can teach these techniques by behaving as a role model and providing formal or informal inservice education addressing the issue of conflict resolution.

Organizing Open Forums

Open forums allow staff to verbalize their problems and concerns, which can lead to creative problem solving. An example of such a forum would be a staff meeting to set up a difficult holiday schedule and to provide the staff with a greater sense of schedule ownership. However, it is important for the manager to make sure such meetings do not turn into gripe sessions with no focus on problem solving.

Using Outside Resources

The nurse manager can also call in outside resources when conflicts or issues arise among the staff. An objective person might help the staff members feel more comfortable and less vulnerable discussing their feelings. A nurse consultant or psychiatric liaison nurse can help the nurse manager recognize and identify problems within the organizational system. Utilizing outside resources can also lead to creative problem solving, positive outcomes, and personal growth.

Offering Educational Programs
Effective coping mechanisms and resilience can be learned. Educational programs can help nursing staff look at themselves and situations in more positive and less critical ways. Possible topics include:

- *Self-talk*—what individuals say to themselves can affect their self-image and the way they handle situations. People can learn to use positive self-talk in place of negative.
- *Life-style management*—staff can develop healthier life-styles through educational programs. These programs can help staff members develop a sense of mastery and control over their environment.
- *Relaxation and guided imagery*—these techniques promote a sense of mastery and control over one's life. Staff can easily learn these effective techniques.
- *Financial planning*—the staff nurse can use financial planning to feel in control of his or her personal life. Learning how to manage money can provide a sense of satisfaction for the staff nurse.
- *Miscellaneous*—often staff will speak about other issues. This can serve as a cue to the nurse manager that a program could prove useful.

□ Conclusion

Unique stressors will confront nursing in the 21st century. The nurse manager's challenge will be to deal with these stressors and at the same time provide a nurturing and growth-oriented environment. The management style that best fits this challenge is characterized by spontaneity, creativity, and flexibility. It demands an understanding of the interactive processes between manager and staff. A manager's ability to provide an environment that fosters autonomy, self-esteem, and creativity will promote physical and emotional resilience and healthy coping mechanisms among staff.

Nurse managers can help their staff manage stress on the unit by understanding the stress process, being able to identify negative stressors, and intervening appropriately. The nurse manager should be able to identify negative coping mechanisms and implement strategies for enhancing adaptive coping behaviors. Finally, the nurse manager can proactively create a culture in which healthy coping mechanisms are fostered.

□ *References*

1. Selye, F. *The Stress of Life.* New York City: McGraw-Hill, 1956.

2. Lazarus, R. *Psychological Stress and the Coping Process.* New York City: McGraw-Hill, 1966.

3. Pollack, Susan. The stress response. *Critical Care Quarterly* Mar. 1984, p. 7.

4. Lazarus.

5. Lazarus.

6. Flach, F. *Resilience: Discovering a New Strength at Times of Stress.* New York City: Fawcett Columbine, 1988.

7. Flach.

8. McCarthy, P. Burnout in psychiatric nursing. *Journal of Advanced Nursing* 10:305–10, July 1985.

9. Storlie, F. Burnout: the elaboration of a concept. *American Journal of Nursing* Dec. 1979, pp. 2108–11.

10. Gribbons, R. E., and Marshall, R. E. Strategies for coping with stress utilized by nurse managers in PICU units. *American Journal of Perinatology* 1(3):268–71, Apr. 1984.

11. McBride, A. B. *Leadership: Developing a Talent for Optimism 1989.* Indianapolis, IN: Indiana School of Nursing and Medical Education Resources Program. [Videotape.]

12. McBride.

13. McBride.

14. McBride.

15. McBride.

Chapter 5

Planning and Developing a Professional Practice Model

James O'Malley, R.N., M.S.,
and Susan Cummings, R.N., M.N.

Rosabeth Moss Kanter, in her acclaimed book *When Giants Learn to Dance,* provides a useful analogy of today's health care industry with the challenges Alice faced in *Alice in Wonderland.*[1] In her croquet game with the Queen-of-Hearts, Alice is compelled to deal with constant change. In that croquet game nothing remains stable for long—everything around Alice is alive and changing. The mallet, a live flamingo, moves its neck and lifts its head just as Alice is going to hit the ball. The ball, a live hedgehog with a mind of its own, does not lay still waiting to be hit. It unrolls, gets up, and moves to another part of the court. On top of all this, the Queen-of-Hearts changes the structure of the game at her whim. When technology is substituted for the flamingo; employees and customers for the hedgehog; and government regulators, the Joint Commission on Accreditation of Healthcare Organizations, and corporate raiders for the queen, Alice's story fits the modern health care industry experience.

☐ The New Health Care Game

It gets harder and harder for the nurse managers and executives who are in Alice's position to succeed by utilizing traditional bureaucratic methods when technology, customer preferences, employee loyalties, and industry regulators are all changing at once. Like Alice, nurse managers, instead of merely keeping their eyes on the ball, must watch all the changing elements. If this analogy holds true, then "winning" or surviving will require managers to be more focused on new opportunities and develop the ability to take action more quickly. Nurse managers will also need to cultivate more friendly partnerships with employees and customers and develop more flexibility by creatively maneuvering events, services, and programs.

This new game in health care brings with it new challenges for managers and executives. Demands will come from every part of the organization and, at times, seem increasingly incompatible and sometimes even impossible. Figure 5-1 describes the changing roles and challenges for both the nurse manager and nurse executive.

Managers and executives will be required to perform the ultimate organizational balancing act. They will be expected to cut back and trim down in some areas and simultaneously grow in others. The organizational battle cry—from nursing services to ancillary and support services to business and administrative services—will continue to be to accomplish more with fewer resources.

The reality for the health care industry is that change will continue to be the only constant. As opportunities further expand, not only will competition continue to heat up among hospitals, but competition among practicing physicians and hospitals will intensify as more services move to the outpatient setting. Health care will continue to grow in complexity, especially along the technological, economical, moral, and ethical constructs.

The traditional structure and cumbersome bureaucracy of most organizations have limited nursing's ability to respond to these changes

Figure 5-1. Changing Roles in Health Care

A. The Nurse Manager

Get "lean and mean" by restructuring programs and services.	⟶	But keep morale up and the employees happy.
Communicate a sense of urgency and push for faster results.	⟶	But use established processes and take time to plan.
Delegate decision making.	⟶	But centralize to capture efficiencies and combine resources.

B. The Nurse Executive

Think and plan strategically—see the big picture and invest in the future.	⟶	But know every detail of the business and do not erode today's bottom line.
Take risks—develop new products and services.	⟶	But do not cost the organization anything by failing.
Speak up—be the leader—have all the answers.	⟶	But be participative and listen well.

in health care. Over the past decade, changes have occurred in technology, reimbursement, length of stay, and human resource availability. Nursing's challenge for the 1990s and beyond is how to best redesign nursing and other clinical delivery systems to ensure high-quality and low-cost outcomes that are responsive to consumer needs, compatible with existing manpower and financial resources, and satisfying for the nursing care provider.

One way institutions can cope with these changes is to restructure health care delivery. Redesigning patient care delivery within the context of a professional practice model is the foundation for managing the cost–quality paradigm. Although there are considerable variations in the definitions of what constitutes a professional practice model, almost all include the following components:

- Standards of practice (for example, JCAHO, American Nurses Association, specialty nursing organizations)
- Nursing theory base (for example, Roy, Orem, Rogers)[2]
- Privileging, credentialing, peer review (for example, specialty nursing organizations, state credentialing)
- Professional development (for example, empowerment, professional practice, career advancement)
- Governance structure (for example, shared governance, decentralized decision making)
- Care delivery system (for example, primary nursing, case management)

More than any other component, the care delivery system drives the clinical and organizational outcomes for patient care. Professional practice models provide the framework for achieving clinical outcomes by positioning the professional nurse as a clinical care coordinator, critical thinker, and autonomous decision maker. Consequently, redesigning the care delivery system in the absence of a professional practice model almost always results in diminished clinical outcomes.

The bureaucratic models of the 1970s and the 1980s are now being replaced by the multifocused and transformational models of the 1990s. The new model transformations include:

- *Moving from a high degree of specialization to multiskilled roles.* To compete effectively as a high-quality and low-cost provider, an organization must address the issues of job and system redesign both within nursing services as well as across the organization as a whole. This requires moving staff from highly specialized to multiskilled roles that cross-train to combine technical skills across two or more traditional specialties. The most common role consolidations occur among nursing services, respiratory therapy, laboratory services, and/or radiology services. This concept, already inherent in rural hospital cultures, needs to be integrated into the structure of larger, urban hospitals. In the 1990s, the use of multiskilled personnel will be part of a health care institution's survival strategy.

- *Moving from task orientation to patient orientation.* Care providers will know not only what is going on with the inpatients; they will also be cross-trained to provide multiple services to a given group of cases. This set-up is very unlike the current system wherein staff members leave their specialized department to perform an isolated task on a patient whose person and needs they do not know. Ultimately, centering services around the patient will result in increased levels of continuity, response time, and patient satisfaction.

- *Moving from labor-intensive systems to increased productivity.* Centering services performed by multiskilled care providers around the patient has significant potential to increase productivity. Studies indicate that highly specialized care providers in current systems, such as electrocardiogram (EKG) technicians, phlebotomists, respiratory therapists, and intravenous (IV) nurses, spend 40 percent of their time in nonproductive activities (waiting for elevators and going to and going from patients, for example). By centering services and resources around the patient and cross-training unit-based staff, significant increases in productivity can be realized.

- *Moving from departmental focus to point-of-service focus.* In many organizations a number of departmental staff all review the same patient record for different data—the quality management coordinator, the utilization review coordinator, the social worker, the discharge planner, the infection control nurse, and the risk management coordinator. Redesigned models frequently involve cross-training individuals to collect data for a defined case load and/or patient care unit.

- *Moving from staff shortages to creative solutions.* Moving away from labor-intensive services helps an organization out of the problem of not having enough qualified health care workers. High levels of specialization adversely affect productivity and the hospital's overall financial performance. In addition, it limits job opportunities. Job redesigns that incorporate multiskilled functions centered around a patient population and integrated within a single role result in increased levels of retention, job satisfaction, and advancement opportunities. The highly specialized, task-oriented departments and the labor-intensive systems that were developed in the 1960s and the 1970s no longer fit within the health care organization of the 1990s.

This chapter presents several models for restructuring patient care delivery and describes the restructuring process, which includes organizational assessment and model development, implementation, and evaluation. Finally, the chapter defines the management roles and key characteristics necessary for implementing the process.

☐ Current Models for Restructuring Patient Care Delivery

An array of new models for patient care delivery has emerged over the past decade. All models redefine the professional role of the nurse. Many incorporate managed care concepts, and many utilize clinical and non-clinical assistive personnel to support professional nursing practice. Most of these initiatives are based on nursing theory and are compatible with staff empowerment models. All of these redesigned models provide the nursing profession with the opportunity to improve patient care and advance professional nursing's contributions to the entire health care system.

Nursing literature is replete with redesign examples that focus on how best to structure delivery systems to provide high-quality and cost-effective nursing services. [See the bibliography at the end of the chapter.] A review of the literature provides insight into traditional, as well as innovative, nursing care delivery and can spark creative genius in adapting existing models or generating new ones. This section offers a brief overview of two model categories: those that employ case management and those that expand the utilization of nurse extenders. This section does not represent an exhaustive list of patient care delivery models. Some institutions have adopted these models; others have created new models applying related principles. An organization's decision must always be based on specific institutional needs and characteristics.

Case Management Models

In a nurse case management system, nurses plan and coordinate clinical care across a continuum of illness to attain clinical and resource management outcomes for both individuals and groups of patients. In these models, the nurse case manager coordinates all aspects of clinical care with the physician and other members of the patient care team. Standards and outcomes translate horizontally and vertically across disciplines within the health care system. Case management strategies are generic in nature and amenable to many organizational designs.[3-8]

Nursing case management systems provide a number of benefits to health care organizations. These benefits include:[9]

- More timely attainment of clinical outcomes
- Promotion of collaborative practice

- Coordination of clinical services
- More appropriate utilization of resources
- Facilitation of timely discharge
- Support for nurse recruitment, retention, and job satisfaction
- Increase in reported patient and physician satisfaction

The following subsections describe three types of case management models—primary nursing, differentiated practice, and community based.

Primary Nursing–Based Case Management

Primary nursing–based case management requires a registered nurse to provide 24-hour care accountability from admission to discharge for a small group of patients on a specific unit.[10] Each registered nurse is assigned a small group of primary patients, usually three to five. The nurses care for their primary patients when they are working and write care plans for when they are off-duty, thereby ensuring that other nurses follow the correct plan of care. As a care delivery system, primary nursing has significantly enhanced patient and nurse satisfaction along with the continuity of care. However, the quality–cost outcomes of this model are marginal.[11]

The methodology of primary nursing case management organizes patient care through an illness episode wherein identified clinical and resource management outcomes are achieved within a specified time frame. In this model, as developed by Zander, critical pathways and case management plans specify time-contingent interdisciplinary processes and outcomes.[12,13] Variances or deviations of the patient's progress toward goal attainment are assessed and documented every eight hours so that appropriate care plan modifications and corrective interventions can be implemented.

Case Management Differentiated Practice

The case management differentiated practice model focuses on managing a patient's care from admission to postdischarge. One of the model's unique characteristics is leveled, or differentiated practice in which there are clearly defined roles for nurses with baccalaureate and associate degrees.[14] This workplace redesign is based primarily on nursing education and includes technical, interpersonal, and management skills related to patient care. Professional and technical roles are implemented on the basis of clearly defined clinical competencies and role expectations reflecting each nurse's basic education, ability, and initiative.

Community-Based Case Management

In community-based case management, a nurse manages and coordinates the entire spectrum of a patient's care irrespective of the setting in which care is provided. The nurse may provide hands-on care and act as a patient advocate and a broker of service to ensure appropriate resource management and quality clinical outcomes. For example, the community-based nurse case management delivery system developed at St. Mary's Carondolet Hospital in Tucson incorporates what is thought to be the first nursing health care management organization (HMO). The HMO delivers care to senior citizens enrolled in a Medicare risk contract program. The nurse case manager oversees patient care, ensures that it is provided in the most economical setting (whether inpatient or outpatient), and helps patients manage self-care and establish linkages with appropriate community agencies.[15]

Nurse Extender Models

The nursing shortage of the 1980s coupled with the high cost of providing health care has led many nurse executives and managers to consider developing nursing care delivery redesigns that more effectively utilize the skills of the professional nurse as well as provide them additional support. These models often utilize nurse extenders (clinical and non-clinical assistive personnel) to enhance the effectiveness and efficiency of the professional nurse in providing high-quality and cost-efficient care.

Primary Practice Partners

The primary practice partner model incorporates a technical assistant as a nurse's partner.[16] Registered nurses select their own primary partners, technical assistants who work the same schedule. Within the partnership, the technical assistant performs delegated duties under the registered nurse's direction. Over time, the nurse expands the partner's responsibilities when he or she determines that the partner is ready. Although this model is effective in utilizing scarce resources to provide high-quality and cost-efficient care, successful implementation depends on the utilization of unlicensed personnel as legislated by each state's nurse practice act.

Licensed Practical/Licensed Vocational Nurses

To some extent, many hospitals still incorporate licensed practical nurse/licensed vocational nurse roles within their systems to support professional nurses in technical aspects of care (such as catheterization, dressing changes, and medication administration, as defined in the state's nurse practice act and regulatory codes). In other settings, today's licensed practical/licensed vocational nurse assumes responsibility for implementing some components of the nursing process, including patient assessment, care planning, implementation, and evaluation.[17]

Professionally Advanced Care Team (ProACT™)

By increasing the use of clinical and nonclinical personnel at the point of care, the professionally advanced care team (ProACT) model[18] successfully utilizes fewer registered nurses in expanded roles. The ProACT model encompasses nursing case management. It provides additional support for professional nurses by reducing their responsibility for the provision of nonskilled/nonnursing tasks. This model separates primary nurse roles and clinical care management roles, utilizes licensed vocational nurses and nurse aides to assist in providing direct care, and expands clinical and nonclinical support services on the unit. Within this system, the clinical care manager focuses on overall clinical and business management during a patient's hospitalization. On a daily basis, a primary nurse coordinates the patient's care directly and a licensed practical nurse functions as an associate nurse practicing under the primary nurse's supervision. Related clinical and support services, including pharmacy, housekeeping, central supply, and dietary, provide unit-based services to better support patient care delivery.

Multiskilled Health Care Workers

Multiskilled health care workers competently complete tasks that cut across two or more paramedical specialties, often including emergency medicine, radiography, clinical laboratory service, electrocardiography, and respiratory therapy.[19] Multiskilled workers' tasks incorporate clinical as well as nonclinical functions such as transportation, shelf stocking, or housekeeping. A central component of most innovative nursing models is the integration of multiskilled roles for both clinically and nonclinically assistive personnel. Although these roles provide additional support to registered nurses, a number of issues need to be resolved within the institutions utilizing this model:

- How are multiskilled workers best trained (for example, through classroom, hands-on, and/or individual instruction)?
- How can multiskilled competencies be defined (for example, based on standards of practice or state nurse practice acts)?
- Who can best supervise these multiskilled workers (for example, staff nurses, charge nurses, or head nurses)?

• What performance evaluation system can be developed and implemented to ensure high-quality and cost-effective patient and organizational outcomes, as well as individual employee development (for example, performance appraisals, written tests, competency assessments, or ongoing monitoring activities)?

One example of a multiskilled health care worker is the *hospitality representative*, a role designed and implemented at Sharp Healthcare in San Diego. A hospitality representative is a staff member on the patient care unit who provides nonclinical support to nursing staff and fulfills the patients' expectations for "personalized consumer-friendly, nonclinical services at the bedside."[20] The hospital representative's role integrates several components of admitting, dietary, housekeeping, and nursing assistant functions. It has successfully centered services around the patient and has decreased specialization in ways that have enhanced productivity and service satisfaction.

☐ The Process for Restructuring Patient Care Delivery

Irrespective of model and role design, there are some typical components common to successful practice transformation associated with patient care redesigns. Executives and managers drive the processes necessary to reshape the environment. It is critical to the redesign's success that the nursing leadership team create a clear organizational vision, provide unfaltering support for organizational change, and most important, be flexible and support high-performing work teams at all levels of the organization.

Generally, there are five sequential steps to successful practice transformation:

1. Goal definition
2. Organizational assessment
3. Model design and development
4. Model implementation
5. Model evaluation

Goal Definition

Before initiating the redesign process, it is imperative that the nurse managers identify clear goals—benchmark measures reflecting successful efforts to improve patient care and redefine professional roles. Although goals for a workplace redesign project need to be organization specific, most support professional nursing practice, high-quality clinical outcomes, enhanced customer satisfaction, and increased productivity and cost reductions.

Goals emanate from the organization's mission, values, philosophy, and strategic and operational plans. Goal setting includes identifying desired outcomes, developing action plans, and establishing measurement criteria. The process for defining goals reflects the organization's culture and structure. In hierarchical bureaucratic organizations, both strategic and operational goals are often determined at the administrative level and implemented throughout the organization. In sociotechnical organizational models, goals for a redesign may be determined by those providing care at the point of service within boundaries (fiscal, material and human resources, and so forth) established by nursing or organizational leadership.

Examples of goals for redesigning the workplace might include:

- Cost per unit of service to be decreased by X dollars
- Productivity to be increased by X percent
- Continuous quality improvement as evidenced by comparison with national benchmarks or internal measures
- Job satisfaction of all caregivers to be increased by X percent
- Physician satisfaction to remain constant or increase

It is important that those individuals with a vested interest in defining a project and its outcomes be involved in goal setting. Key stakeholders usually include representatives of the organization's administration, caregivers, patients and families, third-party payers, and employees who purchase health care services. The nurse managers and nurse executives must create the environment and processes to ensure that the goals and outcome definitions are clear and reflect the vested interests of the prime interest groups. Without the stakeholders' support for change, the redesign will probably not be successful in the long run.

Organizational Assessment

After the nurse manager defines goals, the next step toward model redesign is to perform an organizational assessment. This assessment provides a solid base for planning, monitoring, and evaluating the change process. An organizational assessment ensures that the redesign reflects the organization's mission and values and supports its objectives.

The assessment data provide the framework for identifying issues the redesign process must address. Along with analyzing past and present data, an assessment must factor how future forecasts may affect the workplace restructuring and care delivery redesign process. Knowing where the organization has been, where it is currently, and where it needs to be in the future serves as the nurse manager's prelude for making appropriate decisions about model development.

The organizational assessment includes an internal analysis of controllable factors. The assessment also includes an analysis of external factors (economic trends, technological changes, and reimbursement patterns, and so forth) that are outside an organization's control.[21] Finally, an analysis allows identification of strategic options.

Internal Environmental Assessment

Internal assessments look at factors that an organization can control or change. Internal assessments often focus on an array of operational issues including, but not limited to, the following:

- Technological and human resources capabilities
- Physicians and their medical practice patterns
- Patient origin and market share
- Financial factors, including payer mix, charges, and reimbursement
- Organizational culture as expressed in habits and values

A number of fundamental questions related to the provision of clinical care also need to be answered during the internal assessment; the answers to these questions will ultimately drive the model-building process. These questions may be answered by the nursing leadership team, staff nurses, other caregivers, a project steering committee, or an interdisciplinary task force:

- What do patients expect in terms of care?
- How is the nursing product defined?
- What services are/can be centered around the patient?
- What do nurses value about their roles and jobs?
- What functions/tasks could be accomplished by other caregivers or assistive personnel?
- What are physician expectations related to patient care?
- What nursing resources are available?
- How does the physical design of the unit/hospital affect care delivery?
- What financial and operational systems resources can be allocated to redesign/restructuring and ongoing support of change?

In addition, several issues related to corporate culture also need to be addressed. These questions, which can be answered individually by stakeholders or by a task force representing all interested parties, include the following:

- What behaviors characteristically promote the organization's success?
- What behaviors and skills need to be developed to meet tomorrow's mission?
- Is the organization committed to and ready for a major systems change?

External Environmental Assessment

An external environmental assessment also provides data that will be useful in planning the redesign. Although external assessment factors are not often amenable to change, they must be taken into account. Failure to address them may lead to missed opportunities and compromised outcomes. External factors to be assessed include:

- Economic trends nationally and within the service area
- Projections and factors affecting utilization of services
- Technological changes and equipment requirements
- Competitor analysis related to clinical strengths, services, and consumers' perceptions

Key questions to consider in the analysis usually include these:

- What are the consumers' perceptions of the institution and of nursing?
- What are the competitors' strengths and weaknesses in nursing and patient care delivery systems?
- What changes in technology will affect the redesign?
- What service demographics, utilization patterns, and financial trends have a potential impact on the redesign?

Nurse managers and nurse executives can orchestrate the external trend assessment by collecting, analyzing, and interpreting the data. Much of this information is readily available to them. Useful resources include market research and business development departments in health care organizations, as well as the Health Care Financing Administration, Monitrend, and state health department data.

Identification of Strategic Options

The last step in the assessment phase is to identify strategic options. The strengths, weaknesses, potential opportunities, and threats identified during the internal and external environmental assessments provide nurse managers and nurse executives with information to conceive and form appropriate strategic options. Questions that must be asked to form strategic options include the following:

- What are the benefits of the redesign to the patient, caregiver, physician, and organization?

- What is the feasibility of the redesign in terms of human, material, fiscal, systems, and support services resources?
- How does the redesign fit with the organization's mission, values, and philosophy?
- What might the political repercussions be within the organization?
- What will the effect on competitors be?

Further Definition of Nursing Practice

The changing needs and expectations of the health care consumer, as well as changes in the health care environment (the growth of managed care, increased patient acuities coupled with decreased length of stay, and so forth) not only have affected the value system and culture of nursing but also have served as a catalyst to further define professional nursing practice and build new nursing care delivery systems. These changes have affected three aspects of the health care delivery system: the health care setting, nursing care services, and the professional nurse (see figure 5-2). Following are some questions that need to be considered during the assessment phase of redesign. The discussion of these questions should provide a framework for defining the nursing product and appropriate service delivery systems.

Questions to be asked about the health care setting include these:

- Where is nursing care being provided within the horizontally and vertically integrated health care organization?
- How does the delivery system use the internal culture and external environment to redirect professional practice?
- What systems need to be in place to support a resource-driven model?
- Will the redesigned nursing care delivery system articulate hospital goals, business plans, and organizational structure?

Considerations to be addressed regarding nursing care services include the following:

- How can the nursing product be redefined based on changing patient needs?
- How are health care assistants and other supports utilized to ensure quality and cost outcomes?
- What is the impact of various skill mixes on patient outcomes and costs?
- How can the utilization of registered nurses be maximized?
- Is the service design flexible and amenable to change?

Questions about professional nurses as care providers include these:

- What are the nurses' values related to work?
- What systems need to be in place to empower the professional nurse?

- Are specified levels of practice being achieved? Are the levels acceptable?
- How will hospitals cope with the perceived or actual nursing shortage?

By completing an internal and external assessment, identifying strategic options, and answering questions that further define nursing practice, an organization will have a strong information base for creating its desired future and developing and implementing an action plan to support it.

Figure 5-2. Changes in the Health Care Environment

A. The Setting

Setting	Present	Future
1. Organizational design	Centralized/bureaucratic	Decentralized, information-based organization
2. Service location	Acute inpatient	Ambulatory
3. Service focus	Treatment focused, high technology	Consumer focused, information based
4. Reimbursement	Case mix-fixed reimbursement	Multiple reimbursement system

B. The Service

Nursing Care	Present	Future
1. Service focus	High technology, bionic age	Information based
2. Service image	Care a societal expectation	Different levels of care
3. Product definition	Primary care during a hospitalization	Managed care during a lifetime

C. The Provider

Professional Nurse	Present	Future
1. Supply	Scarce	Shortage
2. Career opportunities	Constrained options for women	Entrepreneurial in multisystem corporations
3. Educational preparation	Institutions of higher learning	Graduate preparation
4. Job satisfaction focus	Direct care	Participation, entrepreneurship
5. Role function	Interdependent, collaborative	Independent professional, specialist

Reprinted, with permission, from O'Malley, C., Loveridge, C., and Cummings, S. The new nursing organization. *Nursing Management* 20(2):32, 1989.

Model Design and Development

Once the organizational assessment has been completed, it is time to design and develop a restructuring model. The model design process utilizes the assessment data to confirm or establish goals and to formulate strategies for attaining identified organizational outcomes. During this phase, nursing leadership should build multilevel support for the redesign. Managers build support by communicating their strong commitment to the redesign through established forums within the organization and informal one-on-one and small-group interactions with key stakeholders (including physicians, caregivers, consumers, and administrators). Model development is divided into two steps: model selection and model building.

Model Selection

One or more task forces composed of staff and management select a workplace redesign model. The purpose of these task forces is to look at the assessment data, review current models, and select a model that aligns with both the goals defined at the outset of the process and the organization's mission, values, and philosophy. The role of nursing management is to coordinate, integrate, and facilitate the process, as well as to ensure appropriate nurse staffing and organizational outcomes.

Model selection usually results in one of the following strategies:

- An established care delivery model is adapted to fit the organizational setting.
- The current care delivery model is redefined.
- A new model is created.

Developing possible alternative models to the initial selection may illuminate options that are not initially obvious but are ultimately the most successful. For example, creative options can come out of clearly identifying advantages and disadvantages of various models and focusing questions on patient requirements, human resources, cost constraints, and quality outcomes. Once alternatives have been identified, the potential positive and negative aspects of each should be evaluated before a decision is made on the best course of action.

Model Building

Once nursing leaders select a model, they can then begin building it. Specific activities that must be accomplished during the model-building phase include designing professional nurse and clinically and nonclinically assistive roles and reconfiguring the patient care delivery system. As registered nurse roles change, all other roles within the patient care delivery system also have the potential to change. Managers need to determine how each clinical and nonclinical role fits into the organizational structure.[22] In addition, the scope of relationships, responsibilities, and accountabilities must be determined for each of the redefined roles within the patient care delivery system. Once roles have been identified and defined, necessary qualifications to succeed in a particular role can be determined. Managers must also determine the resources required to implement the model (including human, financial, facility, and clinical information systems).

In addition, during this process, managers should complete a cost–benefit analysis and develop plans for piloting the care delivery redesign and goal measurement mechanisms. Initial cost–benefit analysis should focus on projected start-up costs, break-even analysis, and reductions in cost per unit of service. Managers should also provide the specific financial data required by their institutions for approval of new programs. Ongoing communication and forums for work group problem solving minimize the impact of the change. In addition, evaluating the impact of work group role changes provides stakeholders feedback about the redesign's effectiveness.

Model building also requires the development of a plan to determine the human resources needed for a new care delivery system. Human resource plans almost always include at least three functional components: task quantification, task assignment, and skill mix ratios and staffing standards.[23]

Task Quantification

Managers should develop a patient care activity list organized by functional categories (feeding, treatments, medications, hygiene, elimination, mobility, behavior, safety, psychosocial, teaching, and so forth). Fixed activities, those that must occur at specific times (for example, administration of medications or timed laboratory work), and variable activities, those that are flexible in nature (for example, bathing or ambulation), must also be determined. Nurse managers formulate average time standards through direct observations, time and motion studies, industry averages, or staff reporting.

For task quantification, nurse managers also need to calculate direct and indirect care requirements. Direct care is defined as care given at the bedside; indirect care as those activities occurring away from the bedside, including charting, transcribing orders, and checking laboratory values. Patient care profiles that very specifically summarize the typical time requirements for patient care activities can be developed.

Task Assignment

The manager's second step in planning human resources redesign is to determine who best can perform each activity (for example, registered nurse, clinically assistive personnel, or nonclinically assistive personnel). Caregivers involved with the proposed redesign should complete a simple questionnaire that identifies patient needs and care activities based on patient care standards. The questionnaire also covers who currently provides the care, who could provide the care, and who could best provide the care. Utilizing this information, managers can then plot task assignments by type of care provider. When determining which patient care activities can be delegated, nurse managers must consider the organization's definition of professional nursing practice and quality, regulatory standards, and accreditation standards. For example, in California licensed vocational nurses may initiate intravenous infusions after completing a certification course. In many other states, however, only registered nurses perform this task. JCAHO standards related to patient assessment and care planning clearly articulate the role of the registered nurse in these processes. Well-articulated performance-based job descriptions serve as vehicles to identify, communicate, and clarify task assignments and roles, as well as serve as tools for performance evaluation.

Skill Mix Ratios and Staffing Standards

Once the decisions about task quantification and assignment have been finalized and plotted, managers can determine skill mix ratios and staffing standards. Skill mix ratios define the percentage of registered nurses and clinically and nonclinically assistive personnel required to provide care for a designated population of patients. Analysis of the unit's patient profiles, including acuity, diagnosis, plan of care, and patient classification, clearly identifies the time direct and indirect patient activities require, as well as the appropriate mix of provider type (for example, professional nurse or health care assistant). On average, the information from 6 to 10 profiles represents the majority of case types admitted to a unit or the specific type of care provided by a clinical service. Nonproductive hours are also added to the patient profile data. Profiles may be modified by acuity or a standard factor to more accurately predict the total time required for care. Developing profile data for major case types in a particular clinical service provides the foundation for appropriate staffing and skill mix determination. A manager and staff can then match incoming patients with their profile, thereby more effectively planning skill mix and staffing requirements by shift. In the final analysis, skill mix determinations may have to be modified in relation to an organization's financial resources, as well as human resources available in the marketplace.

Challenges in Decision Making

Model development requires managers to make some hard decisions about how to increase productivity through decentralizing programs and services while decreasing duplication and overhead costs. Difficult decisions in restructuring the workplace are made in areas including job redesigns, role redefinitions, and patient-centered services. Although the nursing and organization's executive team are ultimately accountable for these decisions, such decisions are often best made by those most directly involved in the overall redesign. Redesign frequently requires that a number of hospital departments be drastically reduced. Fragmented, centralized, and compartmentalized acute care hospital structures will ultimately destroy the hospital's viability. System redesigns can create "immense gains in quality of patient care, renewed joy and satisfaction among those who provide the care, dramatically reduced costs – and a virtually reinvented hospital layout, administration and practice."[24]

Decisions regarding job redesign present nurse managers and staff both challenges and opportunities. What is sacred to the role of the professional nurse must be redefined. Most nursing redesign models have demonstrated that many tasks the registered nurse currently performs could be handled more efficiently and without compromising quality by other levels of caregivers. Each organization must decide what its individual needs are in combining allied health and support service roles.

For example, at Sharp HealthCare, some dietary aide, housekeeping, and nonclinical nursing functions were combined to create a unit-based hospitality host/hostess role. Simultaneously, phlebotomy services, previously part of a lab assistant's job, became an integrated piece of the unit-based nursing assistant role. This example shows how job redesigns can better support nursing by moving services closer to the patient and simultaneously decreasing specialization in ways that increase productivity. However, those involved in the job redesign must break down old departmental boundaries, learn new skills and roles, and become committed to new ways of providing patient care.

Employee recruitment and retention also requires nursing leadership to make hard decisions. However, these difficult decisions need to be perceived as opportunities, not problems. Depending on the employee who is staying or leaving, turnover may be desirable or undesirable. A manager often makes these judgments intuitively. Retaining individuals who are wrong for the unit or organization can be a critical error costing the organization far more in the long run.[25] "The transformed workplace needs individuals who are flexible, who are open to new ideas, who can tolerate ambiguity and who do not need the answer, but can live with a definite maybe."[26]

The answers to the following four questions encapsulate key decisions required in building a professional practice model:

1. What does the patient require?
2. Who can best provide what is needed?
3. Where can the services best be provided?
4. How do they affect clinical, cost, quality, and staff outcomes?

Historically, nurses have provided care, but not with as clear an overall understanding and definition of what care is essential and will produce the most beneficial outcomes. Nurse managers must continue to decide which caregiver is most effective in ensuring the attainment of cost and quality outcomes. Currently, the majority of care previously provided in inpatient settings can be provided in the home, ambulatory settings, and long-term care facilities.

As professional practice models are built, nurse managers must define the best structures and processes to attain outcomes for the patient, organization, and caregivers. Nursing research, program evaluation techniques, and continuous quality improvement processes all facilitate model development. Ultimately, outcomes of practice model redesigns should be planned in ways that enhance quality of service and patient and physician satisfaction and that enrich the staff nurse's work environment at the same time. Redesigns must also be structured to achieve operational and financial effectiveness.

Redesigning the workplace is not about doing more with less; it is about doing things differently to achieve system enhancements. These enhancements provide for more accessible and affordable care, redefine clinical and service delivery outcomes, enhance quality improvements, and strengthen consumer satisfaction.

Model Implementation

The fourth step of the redesign process is implementation. Implementation usually occurs in two steps: a pilot implementation and then a full implementation.

Pilot Implementation

Often, the first phase of implementation involves installing a pilot program on a demonstration unit. The pilot allows for testing role and systems redesign. The pilot also provides the opportunity to both fine-tune the redesign in a clinical setting and determine future directions for redesign. A pilot of 90 to 120 days usually allows the organization ample time to clarify roles and begin the processes necessary to resolve interdisciplinary issues. A pilot program helps determine whether the new roles and relationships among caregivers facilitate attainment of the desired clerical and quality–cost outcomes. The pilot phase also provides stakeholders initial project evaluation.

Several tasks need to be completed prior to actual plot initiation. Nurse managers and executives must select qualified people to fill the new roles. Critical components of redesign also include developing communication and educational strategies and management information systems. Information must be appropriately and effectively disseminated. As in the planning phase, communication and active listening in and to all levels of the organization are imperative to proactive contingency planning. Education is vital for those who will be developing new roles to ensure they have the basic skills and tools to manage patient care within the parameters of the redesign and for those caregivers and nonassistive personnel whose roles will be affected by the change.

The success of the pilot is contingent on role negotiation and clear definition of win–win situations with all disciplines involved in the patient care delivery process. Everyone must agree to and be able to function in their new roles. Information systems for managers and direct caregivers must also support the model. If new or redefined automated systems or manual documentation systems must be developed, they are best completed prior to initiating the pilot.

When overseeing pilot implementation, management and leadership also must ensure that the "job of patient care" gets done. Because not everyone will understand their new roles and responsibilities, managers must provide appropriate direction and assistance. During the implementation phase, the manager and nurse executive must continue to demonstrate their support through open communication. They must be willing to stay on course through tough times and demonstrate sensitivity to human issues. In addition, leadership needs to ensure that the necessary resources continue to be allocated to support the change. Pilot implementation signifies commitment to change and clearly demonstrates the potential strengths and weaknesses of the redesign.

Once a pilot has been initiated, early initial outcome measurements can indicate the level of the project's success. Before full redesign implementation can begin, strategies for improvement need to be identified and implemented. The pilot strengthens and facilitates the redesign's fit within the organization.

Full Implementation

Full implementation mirrors the tasks of the pilot. Special attention is paid to developing the staff, and there are ongoing formative and summative evaluations. Ongoing education and communication at all levels of the organization are prerequisites to full implementation. Lack of information usually leads to redesign failure. During this phase, managers must develop an action plan allowing for contingencies. Problem-solving forums at all levels of the organization are essential for success.

During the pilot phase, nurse managers and nurse executives must ensure that the organization's activities are reprioritized to reflect the change. For example, reallocation of resources, redefined performance appraisal systems, and the creation of forums for problem solving can reflect the organization's commitment to, and signify the importance of, the redesign. By offering motivational rewards, as well as regularly communicating implementation progress to all interest groups, the nurse manager enhances the success of the workplace redesign project.

Model Evaluation

Evaluation—measuring process and outcome variables over time—is critical to a project's success. The most common evaluation approach taken by managers utilizes a program evaluation model. Through systematic research, these models define whether outcomes are being achieved. These models not only provide formative and summative measures of the project's success, but they also identify opportunities for enhancement. These models can be useful in:

- Assessing the need for new programs
- Planning the initial and ongoing model development
- Clarifying the outcomes of the project
- Determining whether programs should continue
- Planning program revisions
- Evaluating process and outcome measures of change
- Solidifying commitment of key interest groups to the project

A frequently utilized program evaluation model is Renzulli's Key Features Model.[27] This model provides a format for investigating all relevant factors bearing directly or indirectly on a program's effectiveness. The major components of the model are key features, prime interest groups, and measurements over time. Key features are the major factors or variables (quality, cost, meeting patient requirements for care, and so forth) that contribute to the success of a program. These features represent the vested interests of individuals who have some direct or indirect interest in the program being evaluated. The underlying assumption is that each group of vested individuals will define the success of the project on the basis of its own interests. As a critical element, measurement over time identifies points in time to make both formative and summative evaluations. These evaluations supply periodic feedback during the change process so that managers can develop and implement design adjustments in a timely manner.

It is important that managers identify the key features of the prime interest groups prior to implementing the planned program change.

Examples of prime interest groups include patients, their families, nursing staff, medical staff, and administration. Some process and outcome variables that these interest groups may choose for evaluation are as follows:

- Patients and their families
  - Satisfaction with care
  - Clinical outcome attainment
  - Follow-up telephone calls
- Caregivers
  - Job satisfaction
  - Professional enrichment and development
  - Professional behaviors
  - Quality outcomes
  - Physician satisfaction
- Administration
  - Costs
  - Productivity
  - Turnover
  - Revenue
  - Resource utilization
  - Outcome measurements
  - Length of stay by diagnosis-related group (DRG) by nurse

The preceding variables represent only *limited* examples of factors to be evaluated in a workplace design project. According to the program evaluation model, these interests are clarified and expanded through ongoing direct communication with the prime interest groups. Managers need to determine methods for evaluating each key feature identified. As with any evaluation process, managers select and develop tools for data collection, perform analysis, make recommendations, and pursue follow-up action plans. By defining how to measure a program's success prior to implementation, the manager can direct the structure and the implementation process itself toward a satisfactory outcome for all interest groups.

Nursing administration can facilitate the evaluation process by clearly defining what data are needed and, whenever possible, utilizing existing available organization data bases. Patient and employee satisfaction, financial and quality assessment, and utilization management information often provide rich sources of data for analysis. The human resources department and nursing faculty often provide assistance in structuring and completing the evaluation process.

Managers should not initiate changes based on evaluation data before 90 to 120 days after initial implementation. This time period allows for changes to be integrated sufficiently enough to provide meaningful data.

Measurement intervals can be determined prior to implementing the project. If outcome measurements reflect that the project has not been successful, managers can make changes to try to turn things around. However, interest groups may decide to terminate the project if outcome measurements do not support their vested interests. Leadership's role is to support and facilitate the evaluation process and ensure ongoing communication of outcomes to all stakeholders at all levels of the organization. Ultimately, accountability for the decisions surrounding the project's future remains with the executive team.

☐ Management for Change

The successful redesign of the workplace as a foundation for a professional practice model is contingent on the ability of nurse executives and nurse managers to link strategic thinking with strong corporate culture. Superior organizational performance is comprised of nothing more than outstanding individual performance. In the final analysis, individual leaders, not organizations, create excellence.

Redesigning the workplace requires a tremendous amount of time and energy, but any motivated individual can learn how to take on the challenge. There are no theoretical formulas or quick fixes — redesign means converting crises into opportunities and shaping vision into reality. A leader's challenge is to be a visionary and yet remain realistic; to be sensitive as well as demanding; and to be both innovative and yet practical.

Most executives do not have the skills needed to transform their organizations. Because their skills are out-of-date, they cannot move their organizations where the organizations need to go.[28] Nurse managers and nurse executives need to make a paradigm shift from a centralized bureaucratic style to a decentralized management style and from an industrial society to an information-based society. They need to become highly skilled at operating amid ambiguity and charting directions in frequently changing waters.

New Administrative Roles

The nursing administrative staff of tomorrow's health care organization will incorporate a number of new provider roles requiring a new menu of knowledge and skills.

Information Broker

In the future, managers will need to broker the often-overwhelming amount of accessible information. The task of nurse executives and their management teams will be to assess key information so that those individuals closest to services and patients can make the best decisions. The transition to decentralized models in the 1990s needs to be supported by the development of new information services and systems that will ensure that data-based decisions are made at the point of care.

Organization Designer

As organization designers, leaders will need to change structures constantly and realign organizations with a minimum of delay. In a brief period of time, nursing organizations have moved from the traditional bureaucratic line structures of the 1970s to the matrix models prevalent in the 1980s. In the 1990s, these models are being replaced by open organizational structures that have no preset lines of communication. Desired outcomes are achieved within the context of these open organizational structures, because all staff are able to communicate, solve problems, and plan directly with whomever they need to in the organization. Not only do the structures need to change, but managers and staff need to change the way they work within the structural context.

Facilitator

As process facilitators, managers need to be clearly focused and solution oriented. They also need to build partnerships with staff that result in greater empowerment and interstaff support. As empowerment facilitators, nurse executives can build a strong organizational culture that encourages risk taking and innovation at all levels.

Pathfinder and Visionary

Strategic analysis of the changing industry, once a planning function in the corporate office, will become an executive management function. Nurse managers and executives will be their own pathfinders. Strategic analysis for managers includes developing the ability to sustain an organization's competitive advantage by satisfying customer needs. Two successful approaches include creatively segmenting customers into distinct groups and detailing the nature of the competitors' operations. Inherent in the strategic analysis process is leadership's ability to capitalize on the organization's strengths by clearly understanding the forces operating in a constantly changing marketplace.

In general, transformational leadership skills are fundamental to the effective management of corporate culture, strategy, and change. Transformational leaders are truly powerful and know how to implement change. These leaders create the vision in the minds and hearts of others.

They see risks as opportunities. They empower staff at all levels of the organization to be creative and innovative. Most important, transformational leaders are masters at managing change. They have the ability to commit people to action and convert followers into leaders. There is a spiritual dimension to this kind of leadership that is founded on trust. Transformational leaders have a sort of magical, charismatic, enlightening quality. They do not force events or control people. Their style is characterized by trust and empowerment and is best seen in their artistic approach to communication. In addition to having a powerful communication style, they are highly visible and accessible. Transformational leaders have the two primary skills needed for moving an organization from a bureaucratic to a transformational management mode—the ability to reframe problems as opportunities and the ability to convert innovative ideas into practice.

A vital issue for every health care organization in the 1990s is whether it can meet the challenge of redesigning its care delivery system. The answer depends on how its executive and management staff perceives the situation. The first step is for leadership to view problems as opportunities. For example, nurse executives must realize that there is no nursing shortage. What exists is a shortage of creative solutions on how to accomplish the professional work of nursing. There are not enough professional registered nurses available in the marketplace today, nor will there be tomorrow if programs and services continue to be staffed at current productivity levels. The current nursing care delivery systems are obsolete and in their present form cannot survive the challenges of the 1990s.

Another skill needed for transformational leadership is creativity, the ability to convert innovative ideas into practice. Only one's imagination limits the possibilities for health care delivery. A creative leader solves problems by reevaluating situations to determine not the limitations, but the possibilities.

Ackoff describes creativity as an idealized redesign process[29] constantly evolving and dynamic. Creative leadership begins by defining where an organization or unit wants to be. With the desired outcomes in mind, managers then use creativity skills to move from the future back to the present, as opposed to the usual processes of moving from the present to the future. According to Ackoff, moving from the future to the present focuses planners on their ultimate objectives and visions, rather than on current barriers, and allows for more creativity in getting to the desired vision or ideal. Creating visions requires the use of both introspection and projection. Introspection facilitates the mental creation of the manager's vision. Projection provides a means for testing that vision before fully committing the organization to it.

As nurses create visions for future care delivery models, they need to surround themselves with visionaries. In creating a blueprint of what nursing organizations could be, two important questions need to be asked:

1. Can you generate the vision for the future of your nursing organization?
2. Can you implement the vision in your organization?

Creating strategic plans for future initiatives requires that there be visionary people at all levels of the organization. Successful organizations need not only individuals who can create and implement the visions organizationwide, but also those who can staff, budget, and finance the visions on a day-to-day basis.

Key Characteristics of Change Managers

There are several key characteristics that are useful in managing change and facilitating the development of professional nursing practice models:[30]

1. *Trusting subordinates.* Generally, if a manager believes in and trusts subordinates, they will go all out for the manager. Conventional management structures with responsibility and authority residing at the top of a pyramid are fast giving way to high-commitment organizations with high-performance teams. A high-performing team's success is based on trust and a partnership among leaders and all levels of their staff.
2. *Remembering to relax and keep cool.* The best leaders excel under fire. How one capitalizes on the opportunities presented in crises is the acid test for true transformational leadership.
3. *Developing a passion for encouraging risk taking.* Effective leaders encourage staff not only to take risks, but also to readily accept error. Fear of failure should never be the reason not to try something new.
4. *Having an obsession for being an expert.* From the transportation aide to the clinical nurse specialist to the executive in the board room, everyone needs to know that the nurse manager knows what they are talking about. Nursing leaders need to do their homework. Staff follow a lot more willingly if they are confident that their leader knows what he or she is doing.
5. *Inviting dissent and creating a little controversy.* Effective organizational leaders create environments where constructive dissent is supported. Nursing staff members are not giving their best if they are afraid to speak up. "The higher you get in an organization, the more important it is to have people who will tell you when you are right or wrong. If you have 'Yes' people, either you or they are redundant."[31]
6. *Developing an ability to simplify.* Leaders should not get done in by the details. Effective leaders can see the global picture and develop

pragmatic solutions to complex issues. They zero in on essentials, are clear about outcomes consistent with desired direction, and they are effective at keeping the details at bay.

☐ Conclusion

The challenge of redesigning care delivery by facilitating the development of professional practice models is at the top of nursing's agenda. Redesigns require the emergence of new processes based on valuing consensus among team members with divergent abilities and viewpoints, as well as sharing power and decision-making responsibilities. Management practices, corporate cultures, and strategies must be transformed if nursing is to successfully meet the challenges of ensuring high-quality and low-cost outcomes, satisfying consumers and nursing care providers, and effectively utilizing available manpower and financial resources. Leaders who take advantage of opportunities to orchestrate effective change will survive and their organizations prosper.

Nurse managers and executives who empower staff within the framework of high-performing work teams will facilitate change management. Teaching and role modeling, delegation, conflict resolution, negotiation, assertiveness, and stress reduction skills enhance both the manager's and the staff's effectiveness in the workplace. Utilizing these new skills, management practices and strategies is imperative in negotiating an organizational transformation that continues to support professional nursing practice and ensure high-quality health care delivery.

☐ *References*

1. Kanter, R. M. *When Giants Learn to Dance.* New York City: Simon and Schuster, 1989.

2. Righl, J., and Rey, C. *Conceptual Models for Nursing Practice.* New York: Appleton Century Crofts, 1980.

3. Cronin, J., and Makelbust, J. Case managed care: capitalizing on the CNS. *Nursing Management* 20(3):38–47, Mar. 1989.

4. Ethridge, P. A nursing HMO: Carondolet St. Mary's experience. *Nursing Management* 22(7):22–26, July 1991.

5. Loveridge, C., Cummings, S., and O'Malley, J. Developing case management in a primary nursing system. *Journal of Nursing Administration* 18(10):36–39, Oct. 1988.

6. Lulavage, A. RN-LPN teams: toward unit nursing case management. *Nursing Management* 22(3):58–61, Mar. 1991.

7. Rogers, M., Riordan, J., and Swindle, D. Community based nursing case management pays off. *Nursing Management* 22(3):30–34, Mar. 1991.

8. Sinnen, M., and Schifalacqua, M. Coordinated care in a community hospital. *Nursing Management* 22(3):38–42, Mar. 1991.

9. O'Malley, J. Nursing case management, Part I: why look at a different model for nursing care delivery? *Aspen's Advisor for Nurse Executives* 3(5):5–6, Feb. 1988.

10. Marram, G. *Primary Nursing: A Model for Individualized Care.* St. Louis: C. V. Mosby, 1974.

11. McClellan, M., and others. From team to primary nursing. *Nursing Management* 18(10):69–71, Oct. 1987.

12. Zander, K. Second generation primary nursing: a new agenda, part II. The strategic management of cost and quality outcomes. *Journal of Nursing Administration* 18(5):23–30, May 1988.

13. Zander, K. Managed care within acute care settings: design and implementation via nursing case management. *Health Care Supervision* 6(2):27–43, Feb. 1988.

14. Koerner, J., Bunkers, L., Nelson, B., and Santeman, K. Implementing differentiated practice: the Sioux Valley Hospital experience. *Journal of Nursing Administration* 19(2):13–21, Feb. 1989.

15. Perry, L. Arizona hospital operating first nursing HMO. *Modern Healthcare* 21(24):66, June 17, 1991.

16. Manthey, M. Primary practice partners: a nurse extender system. *Nursing Management* 19(3):58–59, Mar. 1988.

17. American Hospital Association. *Restructuring the Work Load: Methods and Models to Address the Nursing Shortage.* Chicago: AHA, 1989.

18. Brett, J., and Tongers, M. C. Restructures patient care delivery: evaluation of the ProACT™ model. *Nursing Economics* 8(1):36–44, Jan. 1990.

19. Starrs, C. The multiskilled movement: a new wave for clinical laboratory science? *Clinical Laboratory Science* 2(4):204, July–Aug. 1989.

20. O'Malley, J., and Serpico-Thompson, D. Redesigning roles for patient centered care: the hospital representative. *Journal of Nursing Administration* 22(7/8):30–34, July–Aug. 1992.

21. Coddington, D., and Moore, K. *Market Driven Strategies for Healthcare.* San Francisco: Jossey-Bass, Inc., 1987.

22. Vestal K. Job redesigns: process and product. *Nursing Management* 20(12):26–29, Dec. 1989.

23. O'Malley, J., and Llorente, B. Back to the future: redesigning the workplace. *Nursing Management* 21(10):46–48, Oct. 1990.

24. Weber, D. Six models of patient focused care. *Healthcare Forum Journal* 24(4):23, July–Aug. 1991.

25. del Bueno, D. Warning: retention may be dangerous to your organization's health. *Nursing Economics* 8(4):239–43, July–Aug. 1990.

26. del Bueno, p. 243.

27. Munro, B. A useful model for program evaluation. *Journal of Nursing Administration.* 13(3):23–26, Mar. 1983.

28. Hickman, C., and Silva, M. *Creating Excellence: Managing Corporate Culture, Strategies and Change in the New Age.* New York City: New American Library, 1984.

29. Ackoff, R. The corporate rain dance. *The Wharton Magazine* 2(2):36–41, Winter 1977.

30. Labich, K. The seven keys to business leadership. *Fortune* 118(9):58–62, 64–66, Sept. 1988.

31. Labich, p. 62.

☐ *Bibliography*

American Hospital Association. *Restructuring the Work Load: Methods and Models to Address the Nursing Shortage.* Chicago: AHA, 1989.

Brett, J., and Tongers, M. C. Restructures patient care delivery: evaluation of the ProACT™ model. *Nursing Economics* 8(1):36–44, Jan. 1990.

Cronin, J., and Makelbust, J. Case managed care: capitalizing on the CNS. *Nursing Management* 20(3):38–47, Mar. 1989.

Ethridge, P. A nursing HMO: Carondolet St. Mary's experience. *Nursing Management* 22(7):22–26, July 1991.

Koerner, J., Bunkers, L., Nelson, B., and Santeman, K. Implementing differentiated practice: the Sioux Valley Hospital experience. *Journal of Nursing Administration* 19(2):13–21, Feb. 1989.

Loveridge, C., Cummings, S., and O'Malley, J. Developing case management in a primary nursing system. *Journal of Nursing Administration* 18(10):36–39, Oct. 1988.

Lulavage, A. RN-LPN teams: toward unit nursing case management. *Nursing Management* 22(3):58–61, Mar. 1991.

McClellan, M., and others. From team to primary nursing. *Nursing Management* 18(10):69–71, Oct. 1987.

Manthey, M. Primary practice partners: a nurse extender system. *Nursing Management* 19(3):58–59, Mar. 1988.

Marram, G. *Primary Nursing: A Model for Individualized Care.* St. Louis: C. V. Mosby, 1974.

O'Malley, J. Nursing case management, part I: why look at a different model for nursing care delivery? *Aspen's Advisor for Nurse Executives* 3(5):5–6, Feb. 1988.

O'Malley, J., and Serpico-Thompson, D. Redesigning roles for patient centered care: the hospital representative. *Journal of Nursing Administration* 22(7/8):30–34, July–Aug. 1992.

Perry, L. Arizona hospital operating first nursing HMO. *Modern Healthcare* 21(24):66, June 17, 1991.

Rogers, M., Riordan, J., and Swindle, D. Community based nursing case management pays off. *Nursing Management* 22(3):30–34, Mar. 1991.

Sinnen, M., and Schifalacqua, M. Coordinated care in a community hospital. *Nursing Management* 22(3):38–42, Mar. 1991.

Starrs, C. The multiskilled movement: a new wave for clinical laboratory science? *Clinical Laboratory Science* 2(4):204, July–Aug. 1989.

Zander, K. Managed care within acute care settings: design and implementation via nursing case management. *Health Care Supervision* 6(2):27–43, Feb. 1988.

Zander, K. Second generation primary nursing: a new agenda, part II. The strategic management of cost and quality outcomes. *Journal of Nursing Administration* 18(5):23–30, May 1988.

Additional Books for Nurses

Managing the Chemically Dependent Nurse
A Guide to Identification, Intervention, and Retention

by Anne M. Catanzarite, R.N.

This book provides nurse managers with the tools and techniques to deal effectively with the chemically dependent nurse. The reader will learn to identify nurses who are experiencing problems with drugs and alcohol, to intervene with those nurses and arrange for appropriate treatment and care, to reintegrate recovering nurses into the workplace and effectively monitor their performance, and to establish policies and procedures that will result in consistent management of alcohol and other drug problems in the workplace.

1992. 219 pages, 19 figures.
Catalog No. E99-154200
$45.00 (AHA members, $35.00)

Harmony
Professional Renewal for Nurses

by Catherine D. Buckley and Diane Walker, MSN
The Einstein Consulting Group,
a subsidiary of Albert Einstein Healthcare Foundation

This insightful volume is the result of the experiences and advice of more than 5,000 nurses who attended a series of one-day seminars conducted by the Einstein Consulting Group. A "no-nonsense survival kit for sanity," the book is a practical approach to job satisfaction and the maintenance of emotional balance. It includes basic principles, self-discovery experiences, and how-to materials to integrate practical ideas, skills, and techniques.

1989. 155 pages, 12 figures.
Catalog No. E99-154150
$19.95 (AHA members, $15.95)

To order, call TOLL FREE
1-800-AHA-2626